My Jesus, My Child

Book of Prayers

Dwelling in His Presence

ISBN 978-0-578-73668-6

Artist Samantha Fury www.furycoverdesign.com

Editor Pam Lagomarsino www.abovethepages.com

Cover art by author

Table of Contents

Psalm 46:10
"Be still and know that I am God."

Introduction

Jesus knew I desired to be closer to Him. He gently encouraged me to put away things that were taking my attention so I could come away with Him. The words He spoke to His disciples rang in my ears, "Could you not watch with Me one hour?" (Matthew 26:40 NKJV).

I began to make daily quiet time a priority. As I sat quietly in His presence, He filled me with encouragement, comfort, forgiveness, and His everlasting love.

I pray as you read His words, you draw nearer to Him. Let His love pour over you. Open your heart, lift your hands to the heavens and receive all that He offers you. Come because you love Him. Come because He loves you.

You are so special, a one-of-a-kind masterpiece, created by the hand of God

"You made all the delicate, inner parts of my body and knit me together in my mother's womb." (Psalm 139:14NLT)

Dedication

All praise, honor and credit goes to my Lord and Savior, Jesus Christ! I humbly dedicate this little book to Him.

Acknowledgments

No one helped me more than my awesome husband Greg. He was always willing to assist me, support me and encourage me. Without him this book would never have happened! Thank you. I love you so much!

And my four precious daughters-Lisa, Danielle, Sarah and Mandi. I am beyond blessed to be your mom! For the many times you asked, "What did you do today mom?" Now you know!

And to my amazing sons-in-law Bill, Chris, Jeff, and Rocky – thank you for loving my daughters. What special gifts you are to me!

A special thank you goes to Pam Lagomarsino, my editor and Samantha Fury, my artist/designer. What would I have done without your expertise and loving advise? You're both amazing!

"Your Word Is A Lamp To My Feet And A Light For My Path."

Psalm 119:105

Come Away With Me

"Consider it pure joy, my brothers and sisters, whenever you face trials of many kinds, because you know that the testing of your faith produces perseverance."
James 1:2–3

Joy

My Jesus,

I am trying my hardest to trust You, but I'm confused. I'm weary and tired of this never-ending battle. I thought victory was right around the corner, and it wasn't. It's one thing after another.

My child,

Don't give up. Never give up. Keep moving forward, one step at a time. Open one door, and if it closes, open another. Be persistent and diligent. When things are going well, it's not hard to be joyful, but when they fall apart, is it easy to lose your peace?

Faith is not tested when things are tranquil and mellow. It is tested when your world crumbles. It's a faith battle, and I want you to win. Stand and fight the good fight of faith. You will become stronger as you win one battle after the other. If you lose a skirmish, get up, regroup, and fight the good fight of faith until you have victory. I'm not telling you to be thankful for trial; I'm telling you to praise Me in spite of it.

Your joy is not based on your circumstances; it's based on your relationship with Me. Satan loses when he can't steal your joy.

"Let the peace of Christ rule in your hearts, since as members of one body you were called to peace. And be thankful."
Colossians 3:15

Seeking Direction

My Jesus,

I'm so confused. Why can't it be easier?

My child,

Listen for My still small voice. It will light your path. It may be a whisper you hear deep within your soul. Listen carefully. Give attention to the words I am speaking. Don't miss the opportunity. It may only come around once.

I may warn you of dangers ahead and encourage you to choose another route. I may inspire you to speak a kind word to a lonely person or write a note to an isolated soul.

The way may seem long and hard, but consider I am the way, and I am leading each one individually. Follow the path I set before you closely. If you stumble, a helping hand is there to lift you. I will lift you and support you, and together we will walk through the valley. Have I not said you will have difficulties and afflictions? But My promise is I will deliver you out of them, not some, but all.

"I will instruct you and teach you in the way you should go; I will counsel you with my loving eye on you."
Psalm 32:8

My Word as Your Guide

My Jesus,

I don't know what to do. I am confused and without guidance, traveling to a destination where I've never been. There are so many options.

My child,

Hear and receive My Word. It cannot be shaken, and neither can you if you follow its path and heed My instructions. There is power in My Word, and it's for all who will receive it. All that is necessary is the asking.

Be aware of Satan's schemes. Don't be like a man headed somewhere he has never been. He uses all his knowledge and scans all the roadway signs that seem to point the way. As he begins his journey, he quickly becomes baffled by road signs and forks in the road. He has a map but hasn't checked it for direction. It is hidden away somewhere, and he's not even sure where it is. He can easily become confused and make the wrong decisions when all he had to do was consult the map for guidance.

Don't let that be true of you. Is My Word hidden away, and you wonder where it is? Make a commitment today to put My Word first place in your life, and diligently seek Me. You will be rewarded with greater faith. The things of this world will grow dimmer and dimmer, and the areas you need to overcome will fall by the wayside. You will soon come to know you can do all things through Me.

"God is our refuge and strength, an ever-present help in times of trouble."
Psalm 46:1 (GW)

The Journey

My Jesus,

Why do I so often fall, become tangled up in the difficulties of life? I need Your guidance.

My child,

As they walk along the path of life, a father holds tightly to his little one's hand, keeping his child safe, so he does not wander off. Many dangers are in the world the child cannot see, so the father guides and protects as long as he can. As they go farther on their journey, he gradually releases his grip, allowing the child more freedom. So it is with you, My child. I am continuously and slowly releasing you to make your own decisions. Only I, unlike an earthly father, am constantly walking with you.

There will be many obstacles as we progress along our way. Some only I see, and without your knowledge, I gently direct you around them. Sometimes boulders are far ahead in the path that could hinder your progress and get you off course, which you should avoid. You do not see them, but I do, and I can easily lift you above and over them.

But because of My love, I will never violate your free will, and I must allow you to choose. You stumble over difficulties that could have been avoided. I did not mean for it to happen, and My heart aches for you. Trust is easy when nothing hinders your progress. If there were no hazards to contend with, there would be no need to trust.

Are you sinking in hopelessness? Are you wandering aimlessly in a storm only to get splashed with unrelenting rain every time you try to lift your head? Then reach out to Me. I am but a breath away.

"Because of the LORD's great love, we are not consumed, for His compassions never fail. They are new every morning; great is Your faithfulness."
Lamentations 3:22–23

Begin Again

My Jesus,

I need you now, and yet, I feel so distant from You. I have been wandering caught up in so many things, caught up in the world, and I'm so ashamed. I don't know where to turn if not to You. I fall at Your feet, Jesus.

My child,

Come to Me, lay your head on My shoulder, and let Me comfort you. I speak to you today of My love. All the days of your life, I have been there. I never turned away, though, at times, you did. I was always watching, waiting for you to return. Now is the time to lift your head, raise your hands to Me, and receive all that I have to give you.

Give all to Me. Lay your burdens at My feet. Move on from your past, and don't look back; I am not there. Don't separate from Me, cling to Me. Don't listen to the enemy who shouts at and mocks you and tells you there's no longer any hope.

Listen to Me as I whisper words of love. I do not harbor anger against you, and I long to take you higher than you've ever been. Take My hand as we journey together. I have much to show you. You will accomplish great things as you stay close to Me. So, grip My hand tightly as we walk this journey together.

We will go slowly. I don't want you to miss the little moments along our path. These times are gone quickly and what once was becomes only a memory. Don't miss the fleeting moments.

"He said to her, 'Daughter, your faith has healed you. Go in peace and be freed from your suffering.'"
Mark 5:34

A Place of Rest

My Jesus,

I want so badly to trust You. I know I need You, but I just can't take the first step.

My child,

How I long for your visit, even if you only sit and drink in My presence, not saying a word. I long for the fellowship we once had. Have other things taken the place of your first love?

I know your heart. Deep within, you long for Me, but you fear renewing our relationship. I know your past, and you need to leave it behind because I also know the future. I have wonderful things planned for you when your life is anchored in Me.

Let Me remind you, faith is the direct opposite of fear. There was a woman who reached out despite the crowd to touch My garment. I told her that her faith had healed her. I would say the same to you. Reach out and touch Me.

Where else can you find the rest and peace that is as still as a mountain stream at sunrise? You are like a little dove, flying and flittering in the sky, searching wildly for a place to land. I have a nest all prepared for you, in My arms. There you will find warmth, safety, and comfort away from the world. Hear these words, My child, and come to Me.

I will not knock you out of the sky. My love would not allow it. I will wait for you patiently.

"Whoever dwells in the shelter of the Most High will rest in the shadow of the Almighty. I will say of the Lord, 'He is my refuge and my fortress, my God, in whom I trust.' Surely he will save you from the fowler's snare and from the deadly pestilence."
Psalm 91:1–3

In My Presence

My Jesus,

Why do I feel so far from You? I don't have any peace. I want to serve You, but I so often fail. What can I do?

My child,

I am calling you back to your secret place, that place of dwelling just with Me. You and I, alone, apart from the distractions of the world. Come away from the TV, away from the computer, and away from all the "good" things you must do.

Yes, come away, My child, just you and I alone. It is there, in My presence, that you absorb My love, My comfort, and My compassion and you arise renewed and ready for the tasks before you, and there you will regain your peace. I say to you, force yourself to lay aside the things of the world because they only hinder and pull you down. I, however, long to encourage you and build you up.

Only by spending time with Me will you get to know Me. Do you know an earthly friend only by passing daily and saying "hi"? No, and only by the intimate contact with Me and My Word regularly can you come to know all that I am to you.

12

So, My child, if you've wandered, come back to Me. I am calling you as gently as a mother dove bids her baby birds return to the nest where they can rest and be safe.

"Whoever does not love does not know God, because God is love."
1 John 4:8

An Empty Vessel

My Jesus,

How can I be all You want me to be? I'm not brave, and I get scared sometimes. There are so many needs, and I am not capable of fixing them.

My child,

I'm not asking you to fix them, only share My love. Stay close to Me. Come away to your secret place where I give you rest. Allow Me to refresh and refill you. See yourself as a vessel to be poured out for others. Whatever the need, be ready to meet it just as I would if I were here on earth. By My Spirit within you, I am here.

Stay close to Me. Each day presents many opportunities to share My love. Stay alert. Be watchful. You are to show love to all you come across. Be mindful not to judge. Learn to look below the surface. How could you possibly know what has happened in a person's life, what secrets they hold, or what pain they have endured? Learn to listen with your heart. A person is so much more than meets the eye. What you see on the outside is rarely an indication of what's going on. I do not call you to fix them, simply share My love. How do you know this is not a divine appointment I arranged ahead of time for them? Let My Word only guide your counsel.

So many are quick to offer solutions that only temporarily ease the pain. Only I have the words of life. My heart aches for the lost. So many are looking to the world for answers instead of turning to Me. Show them My love, and I am there, for I am love. My kindness, through you, could lead one to repentance.

"Fear not, for I am with you; be not dismayed, for I am your God;
I will strengthen you, Yes, I will help you,
I will uphold you with my righteous right hand."
Isaiah 41:10 (NKJV)

Awaken

My Jesus,

My desire is to be Your messenger while I am here on earth—the earth created so perfectly by You. I want to share Your love with everyone I meet.

My child,

Do not fear that you have failed Me. You have not. Only, I say to you, be all you can be; you must be renewed daily. Come away, sit quietly before Me. Be filled with all that I am.

As you wait on Me, allow My Holy Spirit to awaken within you. Just as one who comes in out of the cold and absorbs the warmth of a burning fire, as you sit with Me, you absorb My presence, and you will find My presence is all you need. You will receive the strength you need to carry on.

Just be near Me, rest in My arms, and let Me direct your efforts. Be content to sit with Me; listen for My voice as I speak words of love to you.

"So we are Christ's ambassadors; God is making his appeal through us. We speak for Christ when we plead, 'Come back to God!'"
2 Corinthians 5:20 (NLT)

My Heavenly Father

My Jesus

I sit quietly before You. I praise You; I honor You, and I bless You and thank You. I cherish these times of quiet with You. Fill me again to overflowing with Your Spirit so that all I meet will see You, not me. Bless me, Lord, so I may bless others.

My precious child,

I am ever-present, but you, at times, become complacent and let other things take My place. Don't allow this; be ever vigilant guarding our time together. I have much to show you, and the time is short.

You are My ambassador on earth. Come away with Me, sit, and absorb My presence; be still before Me. There is such freedom in knowing who you are, that you go into battle, not in your strength, but Mine, and I have already won.

"But seek first His kingdom and His righteousness, and all these things will be given to you as well."
Matthew 6:33

Choose Life

My Jesus,

Why do I struggle so with finding time to spend with You? I know what Your Word says, and I know what I should do. I loathe myself for not spending time with You daily.

My child,

Quiet time is not for My benefit, but yours. Put aside the cares and worries that so easily beset you. The daily tasks are many and will always remain. Choose Me; seek Me first, and your cares become My cares. Who can give you peace during a storm? Only My Holy Spirit. But you must choose.

I am a jealous God. I want to bless My children in their hour of need, but sadly, many do not look to Me. Only I have the words of life.

I am everything you need. When you are weak, I will give you strength. When you are weary, I will revive you and give you power. Seek Me, wait on Me. Only then will you realize how much I will do through you. I inhabit the praises of My people; let your voice ring out with praises that shake the very gates of Hell.

Remember, through Me, you are victorious. You are My special child. I love you, and I long to live through you. Together, we will soar like the eagle mounts to the heavens. A lost world is waiting.

"Your word is a lamp for my feet, a light on my path."
Psalm 119:105

Last Days

My Jesus,

Help me do what I need to do in these last days. Help me be more aware of those You bring across my path. I want to be a doer of the Word and not a hearer only. I am weak, so inadequate, and sometimes scared.

My child,

Am I not aware of your weaknesses? Did I not fashion you in your mother's womb? When you are weak, remember I am strong, and I will help you. I cannot use those who are prideful and perceive themselves to be self-sufficient.

I say to you, rejoice when it's difficult. It is in hard times when you grow. Learn to rely on Me alone. My power is all you need. One day you will say, "The weaker I was, the stronger I became because Jesus was with me." My desire is that My children know who they are, not in themselves, but in Me.

The time is very short. I long for the lost to come to Me, but I long more for My own children to return to Me. Many have lost their first love and are deceived by the ways of the world. They do not perceive the signs all around them. I have set My prophets in their midst, but they are deaf to the warnings.

Don't be among them. Stay focused on what I have called you to do. Follow the path I have set before you. A light, My Word, will lead you. Consecrate yourself to Me in these last days. As it was with Esther, so it is with you; I have chosen you for such a time as this.

"I have discovered this principle of life—that when I want to do what is right, I inevitably do what is wrong. I love God's law with all my heart. But there is another power within me that is at war with my mind. This power makes me a slave to the sin that is still within me."
Romans 7:21–23 (NLT)

Come Away

My Jesus,

The pull of the world is so strong, ever beckoning me to come away, to escape, to abandon all I have in You. I don't want to be separated from You. I want to be set apart with You, but I am so weak in myself. How can this be?

My child,

I, too, was tempted, so I understand. I did not want to be separated from My Father, so I often escaped, alone, away from the world's distractions. When you feel lost, return to Me. Venture back to the beginning and remember. Remember where you were when I found you and what I saved you from. Get to know Me by coming away with Me. Steal away by yourself, and spend time with Me. Let Me teach you; let Me love you.

I have much to show you, but you won't realize it if you let yourself get caught up in the cares of this world. As you get to know Me and learn My ways, the things of this world will grow dimmer and dimmer. Lay your burdens before Me and wait. Wait with expectation, and wait with hope. I am working in the spiritual realm where you do not see. The pages of Scripture are My story. They are readily available. Read, memorize, and get My Words within your spirit so you can answer any attacks from the enemy.

Be quiet; listen for My still, small voice. Even when you hear nothing, then praise and thank Me in worshipful adoration. These moments of devotion honor Me, and they are times of peace and restoration for you. As you wait on Me, you will renew your strength. Be still and know I am God. As I told Moses: I Am. I am all you need.

"Therefore, there is now no condemnation for those who are in Christ Jesus."
Romans 8:1

Quiet Time

My Jesus,

I am weighed down, carrying the guilt of past sins. Help me, Jesus.

My child,

Are you still carrying the burden of guilt for sins I bore on the cross? Do you not know that when you do, you belittle My sacrifice and discount My love? The uneasiness and conflict you feel are of your own making. If you have repented and turned to Me, there is no condemnation. But there is an enemy who whispers lies to you. Heed him not! He does this to keep you from becoming all that I mean for you to be.

It is of the utmost importance that you stay very close to me, especially in these unsettled times. How easy it is to become weighed down with the cares of this world. This was never My intention. You must see yourself as a light for the world, shinning the way for others out of the darkness.

Be quiet, be still, and be calm. Come away with Me. There is no room for murmuring or complaining. Only praise and thanksgiving should flow from your lips. As praises ring forth, watch as your burdens lift.

Stay in peace. It is my gift to you. Anxiety and fear are of the enemy. Deal with them forcefully. They have no place in you. Then watch and see; I will send others to you knowing they will be helped.

"You will keep in perfect peace those whose minds are steadfast,
because they trust in You."
Isaiah 26:3

Secret Place

My Jesus,

How I long for these quiet times with You! Only You have the words of life I need. Only You know me more intimately than anyone. How can I not come to You? I need Your help, Jesus. Quiet my racing mind. Help me bring every thought into captivity to You.

My child,

The only thing that will calm your troubled mind is to come away with Me. Sit quietly and allow Me to refresh you.

Just as the morning dove calls in the distance, My voice is beckoning you to come. Awake, arise out of your slumber and come. I'm calling you to our secret place, our hiding place, a place of quiet peace. A place reserved for you alone. No one else can enter in; no one else understands our union.

Give yourself completely to Me. Offer your body as a living sacrifice. Renew your mind daily with My Word so your spirit will be refreshed. The only distractions are those you allow in through your mind. As you renew your mind, the distractions will fade in the distance. I love you.

"But Jesus often withdrew to lonely places and prayed."
Luke 5:16

Times of Refreshment

My Jesus,

I know my need is to get away to a quiet place, but I flounder, trying to find the time. I am helpless unless You help me.

My child,

I am ready to help whenever you call on Me. Yes, only in your solitude will you come to really know Me. I have much to teach you. Some things can only be learned when you are hidden away with Me in the shadow of My wings. Get away from the noise, chaos, disorder, and confusion of this life.

Learn a lesson from My life. Many times I went off alone, away from the crowds pressing in on Me, clamoring for My attention. When I went away, I wasn't neglecting them. Rather, I was being refreshed, communing with My Father, listening for His voice. Only He could give Me peace; only He could fill Me with His love so that I could give it to others. So too, you need these precious times so that you can become all I meant for you to be.

"'Martha, Martha,' the Lord answered, 'you are worried and upset about many things, but few things are needed—or indeed only one. Mary has chosen what is better, and it will not be taken away from her.'"
Luke 10:41–42

Heart's Desire

My Jesus,

I yearn for You. My desire is that You always have first place in my life, but so many things need my attention. I struggle as I attempt to meet with You daily. Help me, Jesus.

My child,

I hold you so close to My heart that nothing can ever tear you away. I long for your closeness. Learn a lesson from Mary. She sat at My feet, while Martha was too busy doing good things, yes, but neglecting the greater thing—spending time with Me. I loved Martha as I loved Mary, but Martha missed what she could have had. She, too, could have sat at My feet, learned to know Me in a more intimate way, and listened to what I taught. I was right there with her, and she chose to put other things before Me.

The path that leads to life is narrow. Not everyone finds it—not everyone is looking. The pull of this world is strong and deceiving. The enemy uses many devices to keep you from Me. The distractions and noise of this world are ever beckoning. Listen for My voice urging you to our secret place, a place of quiet and calm known only to you and to me. Come, sit in My presence.

Bow low in worship and praise. Say My name over and over "Jesus, Jesus" until you feel your strength returning. Then, and only then, will you be prepared to meet the day.

"These things I have spoken to you, so that in Me you may have peace. In the world you have tribulation but take courage; I have overcome the world."
John 16:33 (NASB)

Hiding Place

My Jesus,

Cause me to come, to drink deeply of the living water that only You provide. Prepare me for whatever may lie ahead. My hope is in You alone.

My child,

As you stay in daily communion with Me, you become strong. You will be revived and ready for Me to use you. I ask you to stay alert, stay sharp, stay focused, be disciplined, and do not fear. I am here to help you.

The storm clouds are forming. Adversity will come. This is a promise. Remember, you are not to be afraid. Take refuge in the shelter of My wings. Find your security in Me alone. I am your rock. I am your peace.

Walk with Me into the future. Let Me be your hiding place. You renew your strength as you wait on Me. You will be amazed at the height to which you soar. Remember that with Me and through Me, you are no match for any foe!

"In the morning, LORD, you hear my voice; in the morning I lay my requests before you and wait expectantly."
Psalm 5:3

Seek Me Early

My Jesus,

I know I should spend time with You, read my Bible, and pray, but I don't; something always gets in the way. I don't want it to, but it does. I am so frustrated with myself.

My child,

This is one of the enemy's tactics, to get you so busy with other things, you don't have time for Me. Many times they are good things, easy to rationalize away, but the time with Me is lost. Spending time with Me each morning requires discipline. I am with you always. Will you be with Me? If you only knew the benefits of a quiet time, the peace and joy that is yours, and the comfort you can only get from Me, then you would be eager to put in the effort. I need you equipped.

How can you meet the needs of others when you are empty?

We are in a spiritual battle, and the enemy is fully aware that the more time you spend with Me, the greater the threat you will be to him. He will discourage you any way he can.

A seamstress could easily become discouraged while tirelessly organizing the pieces to make a quilt. The patchwork must fit perfectly to make a flawless image. She sews one piece after the other, not seeing the finished product but tirelessly working. Underneath are many ragged edges sewn together to make a one-of-a-kind classic work of art. In fact, the quilt is often made of discarded scraps. Think about these things when you're discouraged.

I have a wonderful plan for you. Place the pieces where you think they should be, and leave the rest to Me. You can't wait for the garden to bloom if you've planted no seeds. The seeds of prayer and praise. I have provided all you need, look to Me.

Special Creation

"You will receive power when the Holy Spirit comes on you."
Acts 1:8

The Gift

My Jesus,

I feel like something is missing. I want to be all that I can for You, but every time I step out, I feel powerless and defeated. Is there something more?

My child,

There is more. Imagine someone gave you a beautifully wrapped present. You were thrilled! You said thank you, hugged it to your chest, and immediately put it on a high shelf. You admired it from afar but never opened it. That gift is My Holy Spirit. He is lying dormant in so many lives.

Many have received My salvation, turning from sin and to God, yet have not received the fullness of My Holy Spirit. As Paul asked the believers in the Book of Acts, "Did you receive the Holy Spirit when you believed?" (Acts 19:2) I'm asking you the same thing.

I want to empower you to do everything I call you to do. You don't have to live with defeat, frustration, and failure. Take the gift off the shelf, open it, and experience all My love, all My power, and all My strength. Receive My Holy Spirit and all that's available to you. It's time to obtain your inheritance. It's been sitting unclaimed in the bank. Ask to be filled, and you will be.

*"Trust in the LORD with all your heart
and lean not on your own understanding."
Proverbs 3:5*

Unfinished Book

My Jesus,

Why is this happening? Why are You so far away? I can't think clearly; there is so much turmoil, I don't understand. This hurts so much. I'm not strong enough to carry this weight.

My child,

You are not strong enough, but you are not alone, I am with you. Even in your darkest moment, even in your pain, My love is surrounding you like the haunting music of *Les Misérables.*

You are lost in a dark place and can't see your way out. You're groping in the dark and not finding the door. Do not allow yourself to become locked in a prison of confusion and fear. Some things you will never understand. Learn to be content with not knowing and believe. My ways are not your ways (Isaiah 55:8). You don't have to understand; just trust My heart. See yourself rising out of the valley of despair and despondency, and embrace what I am doing even though it makes no sense and you do not understand.

This night won't last, tomorrow is coming; it always does. Wait and see, and little by little, we will encounter the future that awaits you. I am the author of the story of your life.

"But you are a chose people, a royal priesthood, a holy nation, God's special possession, that you may declare the praises of him who called you out of darkness into his wonderful light."
1 Peter 2:9

Chosen

My Jesus.

Who am I, that You, the Lord of all creation, should look upon me, should even care? Who am I, that my Lord should consider me? I am not deserving of Your love.

My child,

Many voices are telling you that you'll never be good enough, you have to "do" something spectacular, you are not capable, and you have no training. Your life and your story is all the training you need. I am with you dispensing grace allow the way.

Who are you? You are My special child chosen for a task only you can perform. I have placed you strategically where you are. Only you can reach the people around you. Many are living in the world's darkness. What can you do? You can tell them your story, how you came out of darkness into the light—the light of My love and forgiveness. You can tell them it's available to them. Look to Me.

"This hope is a strong and trustworthy anchor for our souls. It leads us through the curtain into God's inner sanctuary."
Hebrews 6:19 (NLT)

Anchor for My Soul

My Jesus,

My soul is in anguish within me. Please don't allow me to drown in the sea of hopelessness. I'm finding it so hard to trust now. Everything around me is swirling out of control, and I feel like I'm sinking, deeper and deeper into a dark hole.

My child,

Hold on! You will not fail. This is the path I have set before you, and it is the way of blessing, so walk on. Stay close to Me. The winds may blow, and you may drift, but if you're anchored to Me, you won't be lost. But you must cling to Me as one clings to a life raft waiting to be rescued.

Stretch out your hand to Me. No matter how severe the storm, I am here. I will never leave you. I stand right beside you when you are in the midst of the battle. Be unwavering as you cleave to Me. I see your weariness, and I would dry your tears.

Above the sounds of the storm, into the spirit realm, hear My voice calling your name and softly speaking of My love for you.

"If I rise on the wings of the dawn, if I settle on the far side of the sea, even there your hand will guide me, your right hand will hold me fast."
Psalm 139:9–10

My Treasure

My Jesus,

I tremble, thinking what might be ahead of me.

My child,

Do not be afraid; I am with you. Stay close to Me. Hold My hand as we walk through this day, going forward one step at a time. On our journey, imagine that I go before you to clear your path. Imagine I am beside you, whispering words of encouragement and love. Imagine I'm standing behind you to catch you if you should fall.

Do not rush ahead into the unknown, but wait for My instructions. Let My peace be your guide. Stay close to Me in the days ahead. Listen for My voice. You are not alone. You are special, and I love you more than you can imagine!

"Even though I walk through the darkest valley, I will fear no evil,
for You are with me, Your rod and Your staff, they comfort me."
Psalm 23:4

Never Alone

My Jesus,

I'm so confused and grieving now. I'm worn out from crying. My heart is disquieted within me, and I don't know which way to turn. It's like I'm lost in a forest with tall trees all around, hiding the path to safety. I don't feel I can go on or that I even want too. I hunger for Your love and the security of knowing You will never leave me, even if I'm lost in hopelessness. I feel so alone.

My child,

You are never alone. Listen and hear as I speak to you. I am your loving Father who wants only the best for you. Hearken to My voice as it seeps through the towering trees concealing your way out. Rest securely in My arms as I cradle you, safe and secure from the world. Be still and be at peace as you rest safely. Do not be afraid. We will walk through this valley together. I will guard and guide you, and you will be safe.

"Be strong and courageous. Do not be afraid or terrified because of them, for the LORD your God goes with you; he will never leave you nor forsake you."
Deuteronomy 31:6

Wandering

My Jesus,

I'm about to go under! I can't do this anymore. I fell so alone, trapped by this obsession. Why is it so hard? Help me understand.

My child,

My people were enslaved in a culture they were living in. When I set them free, at first, they were grateful, but soon they whined because things were uncomfortable, and the journey was difficult. They had been trapped in Egypt, and they walked into another form of bondage—impatience and complaining. They wanted the easy way out.

Deliverance was long in coming, and they became impatient. They didn't understand My dealings or how the enemies I allowed were to strengthen their resolve and determination. They wanted an easy journey, and it was hard. Do you complain when circumstances are difficult?

Are you enslaved in the culture you're living in? Do you sometimes compromise because it's easier? Are you quietly flirting with the world system, a system I have redeemed you from? Do you complain because you feel trapped by an addiction, a mood, or a compulsion and then blame it on your circumstances? Stop and reflect on what I have already done. There is a table prepared for you in the presence of your enemies (Psalm 23:5).

I am the beginning and the end, and I have My hand on everything you do. If the way seems long and unfair, then remember, I am with you in the middle. I will give you grace for each step, not the whole journey.

Hold My hand as we take each new step.

"'For I know the plans I have for you,' declares the LORD, 'plans to prosper you and not to harm you, plans to give you hope and a future.'"
Jeremiah 29:11

Seek the Promised Land

My Jesus,

When I am stressed by daily living, help me turn to You. I don't want to become discouraged and downcast. I want to be thankful, but I so often become defeated on my journey through life. I turn to You, Jesus.

My child,

As you travel the road of life, don't be like the children of Israel who wandered aimlessly and needlessly for years on their way to the Promised Land. I brought them out of their captivity to bring them into freedom. Slowly, they slipped into a different kind of bondage, the bondage of crying and complaining because they thought their circumstances were too hard. You must trust that I know best.

Don't succumb to the trap of grumbling and complaining. As you travel your journey, be a light in this dark world for a fallen generation. Shine brightly!

My precious child, though a mother may forget her child, I will never forget you. Keep that thought present in your mind, always.

"Consider it pure joy, my brothers and sisters, whenever you face trials of many kinds, because you know that the testing of your faith produces perseverance."
James 1:2–3

Trials and Temptations

My Jesus

I am crying out to You. Save me from myself! Save me from this sin that so easily entraps me.

My child,

If you are struggling today and find yourself in bondage, could it be a self-pitying attitude is enslaving you?

Things did not work out the way you anticipated, and you find you are stuck. You think you can't rise above the circumstances.

You may be entrapped by a sin or an addiction that so easily ambushes you. You feel embroiled in its clutches and can't break free. Somehow, you blame yourself, others, or you blame Me for not helping. This is a snare; I cannot tempt anyone. I am not trying to teach you a lesson. I'm only here for your spiritual growth, encouraging your faith to grow.

Learn to see these discouraging circumstances as opportunities for growth. The roads you travel are no accident. I am using them to refine and strengthen you.

Look for rest areas I provide along the way. Do not pass by them too quickly, or you will miss the blessing that awaits you. They can be hidden if you're not watching for them. A friend who reaches out with an encouraging word, maybe a song that ministers strength and health, or a sermon that offers hope with a word that was "just for you." I planned all these things to help you pass the test.

I love you, My special child. I am for you, not against you. Be blessed!

"Come to me, all you who are weary and burdened, and I will give you rest."
Matthew 11:28

Be At Rest

My Jesus,

I feel like I've been crushed while being sifted through the wringer of life. This life is more than I can handle, and I am weak and weary.

My child,

Come close to Me and rest. The burden you are carrying is weighing you down. Drop it and enter My presence. Step onto a new path with Me as your guide. I will quietly lead you into green pastures beside restful waters, where you can sit and renew your strength.

I know your needs better than you do. You think if you were better organized, things would fall more easily into place. You think if you had fewer responsibilities, you would have more time. You think if only there was no deadline to meet, you would be at peace.

Listen as I speak words of wisdom to you. What you need is more time with Me. You need the peace and strength that only I can give. Take time to renew yourself daily with Me. Only when you spend time with Me in solitude, can I minister to you so that you can love and care for others. This love will not be forced. It will be an impromptu overflow of our communion, our time together. You will only be able to minister and meet the needs of others because of your time with Me.

But most important, my child, I am concerned about your welfare. There are so many needs every day; you could not possibly meet them all. Without Me, you will burn yourself out trying. This is a trick of the enemy to get you so fatigued and worn out you doubt your self-worth. Only when you sit with Me in solitude and stillness and allow Me to comfort and love you, will you drown out the lies of the enemy and the voices of men who scream at you daily.

I say to you: you are not weak but strong. Look to Me, and do not fear. Be anxious for nothing but praise Me in all. Take My hand, and I will gently lead you down a path I prepared in advance only for you. Come away with Me and rest.

"Woe to the man who fights with his Creator. Does the pot argue with its maker? Does the clay dispute with him who forms it, saying, 'Stop, you're doing it wrong!' or the pot exclaim, 'How clumsy can you be!'?"
Isaiah 45:9 (TLB)

Mosaic

Oh, Jesus,

I am so sad. My life has been shattered into a million pieces. I am exhausted and emotionally defeated. I feel like I'm fading into nothingness, drifting into the abyss. Help me, Jesus; I can barely hold on. I need to know You still love me. Do You still care?

My precious child,

Nothing you could ever say or do would diminish My love for you. You are My special child. Never doubt My love. Imagine your life as a mosaic, uniquely fashioned by broken pieces of glass. These damaged pieces were once beautiful, but when they broke, they were deemed useless. Presumed to have no purpose, they were thrown into the trash and forgotten.

You may think this describes you. There have been many hard, painful circumstances, like the broken pieces and the shattered glass that have made up your life. But I say to you, be at peace, My child. I, the Master Artist, quietly bend down to pick up the broken pieces. I place them perfectly into the art I am creating to make you an original piece of art. Don't ask Me what I am making or tell Me how to create.

48

Don't say My mosaic is too jagged over here, or there should be more color over there. Only I have the master plan.

Your job is to stay yielded in My hands and remember the great love I have for you—the kind of love that never fails. Today is the day we will begin again.

"I praise You because I am fearfully and wonderfully made"
Psalm 139:14

Masterpiece

My Jesus,

I want to be all I can be for You

My child,

Dig deep for the hidden treasures of the heart. Learn to look below the surface. A man is so much more than meets the eye. Many times, there are hidden tears yet to be cried, wounds so deep they need to be skillfully excised to avoid hemorrhaging the heart.

Pray and wait. Pray silently even as you're ministering to others, gently leading them through their valley. Each person is a multifaceted diamond, a priceless masterpiece, a treasure that needs to be mined and polished before the true beauty can shine through. See Me as the Master Craftsman, scraping away the rough edges, gently polishing with words of love, encouragement, and hope.

To you, My child, I speak words of love. I am beside you as you travel through this life, I will never leave you or forsake you. Never submit to feelings of inadequacy. With Me, you are more than able, an overcomer. You are a light in the darkness, drawing others to Me. Remember, I am with you always. You are never alone. I am guiding and teaching you as we walk through life ministering to lost souls.

Stay very close. Draw strength from Me daily. I am with you always.

"Look at the birds of the air; they do not sow or reap or store away in barns, and yet your heavenly Father feeds them. Are you not much more valuable than they?"
Matthew 6:26

Uniquely Fashioned

My Jesus,

As I gaze into the night sky and see the stars shimmering and twinkling so brightly, I stand in amazement. I realize I see only a small portion of what You have made. Your greatness is beyond understanding! I am so humbled. Who am I that You should be mindful of me? I fall to my knees with thanksgiving and praise, and I worship You.

My child,

The universe is a wonder, flawlessly formed and executed according to My plan, but it is nothing when compared to you. You are unique, one-of-a-kind, and fashioned by My hand. I created you perfectly, and I have an awesome plan for your life. It is a plan no one else can carry out. It is unfolding day by day, minute by minute as you walk with Me.

Don't ever think I don't care about you, or you have nothing to offer; that is a lie of the enemy. You are My child, and I love you. Your needs are My needs. What concerns you, concerns Me.

Simply listen to the birds chirping. They call out to each other as they effortlessly fleet from one branch to another, knowing I have already provided their food. It is there for them to find. Learn a lesson as you watch the birds. I don't come down and hand-feed them; they must put forth an effort. They search, they trust, and they find. So too, with you.

Open your eyes and see all that awaits you. Step out in faith. If I care for the birds, how much more will I care for you? Think on these things.

"You are my strength, I watch for you; you, God, are my fortress."
Psalm 59:9

On To Victory

My Jesus,

I am weary and exhausted. I don't think I can go on another day. My strength is gone. I feel defeated. I watch for You, oh Lord. Come quickly to help me.

My child,

I see how hard you have labored, and I understand. But you are not defeated!

Arise in my power—stand against discouragement and defeat. You have been made to prevail over the enemy, and your youth is renewed like the eagle. See yourself that way. The enemy is defeated—REMIND HIM! You have been through so much for so long; now is not the time to rest—it's the time to rise up, declare who you are, and move forward. I am with you, and I love you.

"And we know that in all things God works for the good of those who love him, who have been called according to his purpose."
Romans 8:28

Your Purpose

My Jesus,

You have said, "I am the way, the truth, and the life." What do these words mean for me?"

My child,

I am your way. My Word lights the path in front of you. The light will grow dim as you stray from the path so, follow closely. See Me as your guide, leading you through life. A life so filled with My presence that nothing disturbs you because you know I will make a way where there seems to be no way.

I am not "a" truth; I am the only truth. I am your truth. Do not let the popular opinions of the day lead you astray. Guard against them seeping into your thinking; guard your heart. As the world becomes darker and darker, you must grow more and more unwavering in your belief in your convictions. You are not of the world; you are merely passing through.

You belong to another kingdom—you belong to Me! Rejoice in each new day—it is My gift to you. I am life—I am your life. And I came that you might have an abundant life—a life that far exceeds anything the world offers. It is a life filled with contentment, a life consumed with love, and a life overflowing with a peace that surpasses all understanding—a peace the world cannot comprehend. This is my purpose for you—My way, My truth, My life. There is no other.

*"For we are God's handiwork, created in Christ Jesus to do good
works, which God prepared in advance for us to do."*
Ephesians 2:10

Sculpture

My Jesus,

There has got to be an easier way. I hate this; I never thought it
would turn out like this, especially after all the prayers and fasting. I
don't want to give in to feeling sorry for myself, but I'm right on the
verge. I know You know all things and could have made it happen
effortlessly. That's what hurts the most. Why, Jesus, why?

My child,

I am forming a magnificent sculpture. As I chisel off the rough
edges, it hurts as I am doing away with the imperfections of egotism
and pride. I am forming something beautiful. Many times
disappointment and discouragement are part of the process. Just as a
sculptor molds, carves, and chisels to make art out of a piece of clay,
I am molding you.

Trust Me when you don't understand. I have a greater purpose
than your comfort. Getting what you want, when you want it is not
always best for you. Allow your faith to grow as you wait expectantly
for Me, trusting I have a greater plan.

Just as Martha and Mary had to wait, they were disappointed
when I delayed My coming. They must have wondered why,

especially since they knew I loved Lazarus and could have saved him. They didn't understand. All the while, I had a much greater good in mind.

Remember, you are not alone. In your darkest hour, I will shine a light on your path, and I will walk with you, step-by-step. I may not take you out of your difficulty, but I will always be with you to show you the way. These are the times you learn to trust Me. Don't burden yourself down with the cares of this world. Don't give anxiety a foothold. My kindness is forever; My grace and love for you are never-ending and limitless.

"Do not conform to the pattern of this world but be transformed by the renewing of your mind. Then you will be able to test and approve what God's will is—his good, pleasing and perfect will."
Romans 12:2

Shame

My Jesus,

I'm so ashamed. I've fallen again. I didn't see it coming, and I succumbed to temptation. Help me number my days. My hope is in You. Save me from my sin.

My child,

The battlefield is in your mind. The tormenter will remind you of every time you failed and every disappointing thing you ever did. He's the one who wants to keep you miserable and trapped. That's why you must renew your mind with the Word of God. If you don't, then don't think you won't become conformed to this world. The trouble is, you won't recognize it. It happens little by little, a compromise here and there, and before you know it, you have been deceived. Some things can seem so right, but they are so wrong. In My kingdom are no gray areas. There are only absolutes.

The world will entrap you into believing its lies. I am calling you to a holy walk. If you have fallen, don't give in to defeat. Get up and walk again. Allow Me to set your feet on higher ground. You have been vindicated, and you're free. You will be a witness for My grace and forgiveness. You are treasured and priceless, a one in a million creation.

Reflect My Light

"Peter replied, 'Repent and be baptized, every one of you, in the name of Jesus Christ for the forgiveness of your sins. And you will receive the gift of the Holy Spirit.'"
Acts 2:38

Step Out

My Jesus,

I want the gifts You offer: forgiveness and peace, especially peace, but I'm scared. I'm afraid of what's around the corner if I journey with You. I guess I don't want to give up the security of life as I know it.

My child,

Do not be afraid. Imagine someone comes to your door and presents you with a beautiful gift. It has been wrapped with the finest care, a gorgeous bow balances on top. You are thrilled. You hug the gift to your heart, say thank you, and immediately put it high on the shelf, where you can admire it from afar, but you never open it to experience what's inside.

That's what it's like when I offer you the gift of My Holy Spirit. I'm offering not only forgiveness of your sins, but incredible power that you could never have imagined. I offer a love that's unconditional, joy that's unspeakable, patience that's constant in all circumstances, kindness, and self-control in the face of adversity, and peace you thought was unattainable. It's all waiting for you.

Reach for My package and open it. Like a garden, it's alive with many blossoms. Step into My meadow and pick the flowers.

"I am the true vine, and My Father is the gardener."
John 15:1

Vine and Branches

My Jesus,

Help my faith to grow as it should, so I can be all I can for You. What can I do? I want to come up higher, but sometimes, climbing the mountain toward You is steep; I fall, and it hurts!

My child,

My Father tenderly cares for you, watering, pruning, and cultivating so that you bear the choicest fruit. Your job is to stay intimately connected to Me, the vine, to grow and produce. My Father provides sunshine and rain, so you will have the necessary fuel for growth.

Stay in My presence and allow the warmth of My love (the sunshine) to strengthen and help you grow. Allow the drops of rain (the reading of My Word) to fall gently into your heart, to nourish you and provide you with the strength you need. My Father also cuts away what you do not need in your life—anything impeding your growth. He is shaping you into all you can be.

Just as a rose bush is trimmed of dead flowers to make room for the delicate buds forming, so too, you are trimmed of the dead works holding you back from becoming all you were created to be. Like a gardener, He is digging up the weeds that impede your growth, the weeds of selfishness, pride, temper, anything that, if allowed to stay, would strangle the fruit.

Cling to Me during the pruning process, which can be painful. Hold on, stand firm, and abide in Me. Whatever you are going through, I am with you, perfecting the fruit of the Spirit, which is already within you. My Father is arranging a beautiful bouquet of love, joy, peace, patience, kindness, goodness, faithfulness, gentleness, and self-control. The fruits of the Spirit are blossoming forth.

"Your beginnings will seem humble, so prosperous will your future be."
Job 8:7

Grace for the Journey

My Jesus,

Give me the grace to allow You to carry my burdens, my worries, and my sorrows. They weigh me down, and I'm about to fall under the weight of it all. I can't do this.

My child,

I see you are struggling, and My heart is filled with compassion. Listen as I speak to you. As you make your way to your final destination, you are weighed down with regret over past mistakes, holding on to grief and discouragement and sins I forgave long ago. This only impedes your journey forward, causing you to stumble.

There are things you clasp so tightly they are becoming a burden, hindering your course, your advancement on the highway of life. You're trying to carry them, trying to pull them along with you, and they are too heavy for you.

Just as you would check your baggage with an attendant before a flight, check your burdens with Me, release your grasp, and let go, let go of the past. You can't change it; why are you dragging it with you? It's time for a new beginning.

"Be still before the LORD
and wait patiently for him;
do not fret when people succeed in their ways,
when they carry out their wicked schemes."
Psalm 37:7

Evildoers

My Jesus,

Why does evil abound? Why do the wicked prevail? I'm sad and angry when I see all the corruption on the earth You created. Don't let the evildoers succeed. They don't look to You; they only look to the world.

My child,

Do not fret because of evil men. Be still, come into My presence, and let me calm you. Find your refuge in Me and trust Me. Do not envy those who do wrong. Stay far away from evil and resist anger; it only leads to ruin. Commit your way to Me, continue to do good while traveling along the path I have set before you.

There will be many obstacles along your path; the enemy arranged to trip you up, discourage you, keep you from your destination, and entice you to the other side—the dark side of life where you do not belong. You might have to go slower than you thought, but keep moving. There is a resting place at your journey's end. I am waiting for you.

"Going a little farther, he fell with his face to the ground and prayed, 'My Father, if it is possible, may this cup be taken from Me. Yet not as I will, but as You will.'"
Matthew 26:39

I'm Hurting

My Jesus,

I'm swirling in the sea of my emotions. I can't believe this is happening. I have no control. I know my faith is being strengthened, but I don't want this. Isn't there any other way? I'm like a tiny boat drifting in a vast ocean, lost and abandoned.

My child,

In preparing Him for what I knew was to come, I led Jesus to the desert. He needed to know He could conquer and withstand the pressure before Him. Only through hardships could He have learned this lesson. The enemy ever lies waiting to trip you up and spoil the plans I have for you. Be alert, wise to his devices. Stop him at every turn.

You must stay close to Me, enclosed in by My protection, covered with My blood.

*"And [he] sent out a raven, and it kept flying back and forth until
the water had dried up from the earth."*
Genesis 8:7

The Raven

My Jesus,

I have drifted so far from You; I don't know if I can find my way
home or if You would even take me back. I'm a stranger in the land.

My child,

Come back to Me. You have wandered far and wide, searching
for peace and love, and you are weary. In your straying, you have only
distanced yourself from Me.

Think about the story of Noah. When the ark finally rested upon
the mountains, Noah sent forth a raven to seek dry land. The raven
flew here and there, apparently feeding and resting on lifeless things,
never to return to the ark. He was satisfied with the fallen world. He
was content to feed on dead things. He rejected the love and bond with
Noah that I had provided.

But when Noah sent forth a dove, she searched high and low for
dry land and not wanting to feed on dead things; she returned to the
ark. Noah stretched out his hand and drew the dove back to himself.
Just as Noah waited for the dove to return, I wait for you.

"Come out from them and be separate, says the Lord. Touch no unclean thing, and I will receive you."
2 Corinthians 6:17

Be Separate

My Jesus,

I know when I sin, I'm hurting You, and I'm hurting myself more. I want so desperately to be a good witness for You.

My child,

My heart is grieved. My people have so intermingled with the world that I can hardly tell them apart. They do not know what they are doing. Remember, I have told you to come out from the world? I do not say that to withhold anything from you, but rather to keep you from destruction.

There is a subtle danger in compromise, and Satan is the master deceiver. Stay aware! Listen for his lies. There is a better way: drench yourself in the truth; it will set you on the path to freedom. My Word is truth.

A small step off the narrow path can lead to compromise, deception, and finally, a slow, spiritual death. If you comply with the world's ways long enough, your heart will slowly grow cold. Remember who you are. You do not belong to the world any more than I did.

Because you are Mine, the world hates you. You are a light in a dark world, illuminating evil. Men don't want the light because it exposes their evil deeds. They choose to live in darkness, but you must separate yourself from the world's ways and turn to something stronger: My Word. Let My Word separate you from the things of the world to the things I offer.

Go forth in life and live by faith. You are stronger than you think, and I am here to strengthen you. I have asked the Father to keep you safe from the evil one, to set you apart, and to consecrate you with the truth. My Word is that truth. That is why it is so important to spend time with Me—to come away and be separate from all your activities.

Worship Me for who I am, praise Me for My glory, and let My Word become your guide and a light for your path, daily.

"But the fruit of the Spirit is love, joy, peace, longsuffering, kindness, goodness, faithfulness, gentleness, self-control. Against such there is no law."

Galatians 5:22–23 (NKJV)

Little Foxes

My Jesus,

I want to be more like You. What can You tell me that will help me grow spiritually?

My child,

I am the vine from which fruit grows. Be careful not to neglect the little foxes, the little sins that seek to spoil the vine. The enemy will tell you these sins are no big deal. He'll whisper that everyone does it and not to worry, nobody is watching. If you rationalize and listen to his lies, you will soon conform to this world, and then spiral has begun. The next thing he does is condemn you for doing the very thing he told you was no big deal!

Listen, My child, as I speak to you; I am always watching you. Those "little foxes" are a big deal. They are a hindrance to your spiritual growth.

Keep this always in the forefront of your mind: I do not watch you to judge you. That uneasiness you feel is a good thing—it's My Spirit seeking to encourage you to come up higher spiritually.

Be hard on yourself, but do not condemn yourself. This life is a journey with many obstacles along your path. If you stumble, get up, look straight ahead, and keep on walking. Have the same attitude as Paul when he said, "But one thing I do: Forgetting what is behind and straining toward what is ahead. I press on toward the goal" (Philippians 3:13–14).

Remember, My Holy Spirit is always available to help you, guide you, and comfort you. Be at peace, My child. I love you.

"He answered, 'Love the Lord your God with all your heart and with all your soul and with all your strength and with all your mind'; and, 'Love your neighbor as yourself.'"
Luke 10:27

Hidden Treasures

My Jesus,

Open my eyes to see the needs around me! Help me love as You love!

My child,

Never judge a person by what you see on the outside. A beautiful pearl lies hidden beneath the rugged, outward shell of the oyster. Diamonds are mined deep within the earth; a plain moth becomes a beautiful butterfly.

So many people are thrown into a trash heap of life and forgotten. Some are wandering aimlessly through the clutter and chaos, unnoticed, thinking they have no worth. Many people, like unopened gifts, are put high on a shelf and forgotten, their potential never to be realized.

My heart aches for My forgotten children. Many cannot relate to a loving Father, and I long to stand in the gap for them, to be the father they never had. I long to tell them how very special they are, that they can succeed and they can be even more than they thought they could.

I ask you, My child, to tell them they can make it, despite what they have been through. Tell them I love them, that they can become greater than they can even imagine. Hurting people are everywhere. Open your spiritual eyes to see them. Don't walk by like the religious people in the parable of the Good Samaritan. Count it a privilege that I have chosen you to uncover the hidden treasures of their hearts.

"You Lord, are forgiving and good, abounding in love to all who call to You."
Psalm 86:5

A Light in the Darkness

My Jesus,

I want to be used by You, but I am weak and hesitant to speak. Help me, Jesus.

My child,

This day is My gift to you. Will you use it wisely, taking full advantage of what I set before you, or will you look back at the end of the day with regret at the many missed opportunities? Do you not know I will ask nothing of you that I have not already equipped you to do? Don't say you're not prepared. You have all you need because My Spirit lives within you.

My Spirit is love—love for the telemarketer who interrupts your dinner, love for the Mormon missionary who knocks at your door, and love for the tattooed biker you assume has nothing in common with you.

So many are lost like a man deep within a forest, searching for a way out. He is helpless and hopeless. See yourself as his rescuer, shining a light on the path in the darkness that leads to freedom. My Word is that light for his path. When he finds the Word, he's introduced to Me, maybe for the first time because My Word and I are one.

"Truly I tell you, anyone who gives you a cup of water in my name because you belong to the Messiah will certainly not lose their reward."
Mark 9:41

Be Aware

My Jesus,

My desire is to do Your will. This day, I humbly offer You my life. Show me, Jesus, what to do. Without You, I am nothing.

My child,

I am honored by your willingness and devotion. This then is My assignment for you: be more aware of your surroundings.

People everywhere are starving for encouragement. Many are so beaten down by the world; they feel they can't take another step. They need to hear from Me, but so many ears are closed to My voice.

I am speaking, but I am speaking through you. Be looking for simple ways to be a blessing and to show My compassion and My love. Offer a kind word and a smile. Be there. Listen. Really listen. Your presence speaks volumes.

There are people in your world who need you, many only you can touch. They are wandering like sheep without a shepherd. They are drifting aimlessly through life like a man on a raft, lost at sea. So, stay alert. Be watchful. Be vigilant.

Together, we will lead them safely home.

"Create in me a pure heart, O God, and renew a steadfast spirit within me."
Psalm 51:10

Pure Heart

My Jesus,

How can I be all that You want me to be? Tell me what to do, and I will obey.

My child,

Rid yourself of anything that distracts you from completing the mission I have for you. Just as an athlete disciplines his body, you too, must always be sharp, prepared, and ready. Purge impurities from your life. Be hard on yourself.

Think of a surgeon. Even though he has skill and knowledge, he is required to scrub and do a thorough cleansing before every operation. He needs to wash away any impurities that would hinder the outcome. So too, with you. You must search your heart and check your motives. Do you have preconceived ideas that could hinder the work I want to do? Do not be quick to judge others.

Remember, man looks at the outward appearance, but I see the heart, a heart that may have been injured by the circumstances of life—a heart crying out for understanding and acceptance. A heart longing to be loved. Learn to look below the surface. The harsh actions may be but a snapshot of the hurt that lies within.

Many opportunities await you, so move slowly and deliberately through your day. Come to Me often and seek a fresh anointing. Pray for guidance, pray for wisdom, and pray for love, and you shall have them. I long to bless My children.

"Go after a life of love as if your life depended on it—because it does."
1 Corinthians 14:1 (MSG)

Infinite Love

My Jesus,

I am nothing without You. I need You in my life, more today than ever. Speak to me, Jesus. I am listening.

My child,

I speak to you today of love. My love for you is boundless, and I long to bless you. So come to Me. Lay your requests on My altar, worship Me, praise Me, and go on your way, knowing I will deal with each one in the most loving way possible because I am love.

Think of the miracles I did when I walked the earth. I never turned anyone away, but some did not receive them because of their unbelief. I am the same today as I was then. I am the same yesterday, today, and forever.

Come to Me. Seek Me. I have many gifts to give. Ask Me for the best gifts, and let love be your aim. Pray that My love so fills you that it overflows into the lives of all you meet. This is My desire: that all would know of My love.

"Physical training is good, but training for godliness is much better, promising benefits in this life and in the life to come."
1 Timothy 4:8 (NLT)

Strong in Him

My Jesus,

I want my life to honor You. What can I do to bring You glory?

My child,

You must be sharp and ready for all that lies ahead. A soldier is always preparing for battle. Likewise, you, too, must always be ready. Think of your life as a boot camp where you are being trained, molded, and shaped.

I am preparing, renewing, and equipping you so that you may successfully stand against the enemy no matter which struggles you face. It may be a spiritual battle requiring long hours of prayer and fasting. It may be a solitary battle where you fight loneliness and sadness. It may be an emotional battle where you must war against all the thoughts coming against you.

At times, My love requires Me to hide you away—to shield you from the world's chatter. Then you will learn to focus on things that matter. In your solitude, if you start to doubt My love, run immediately to My Word as a person would run for shelter in a rainstorm. Immerse yourself in My promises.

Think about where you were when I found you. Did I punish for the wrongs you had done, or did I welcome you home with arms outstretched to meet you? A tactic of the enemy is to get you to question My love. If you aren't convinced of My love for you, how can you confidently tell others? So, I say to you, welcome these times of training.

"The LORD is compassionate and gracious, slow to anger, abounding in love."
Psalm 103:8

Little Things

My Jesus,

My hands are weak, and my feet stumble. I am fearful, and anxiety has overtaken me. I cannot see beyond my pain. I feel uneasy in my heart.

My child,

That uneasy feeling is My Holy Spirit urging you on to greater heights. Seek to be aware of what's around you—the little things that are so easily taken for granted—the sunshine on your face, the clean water you drink, and the starlit sky night that lights up the heavens.

The quickest way to overcome anxiety is by prayer and thanksgiving in all circumstances. "Be joyful always" is not just a suggestion—it's for your benefit. Joy elevates you and affects everyone around you.

Remember, just as joy is infectious, so is self-pity and a melancholy mood. Permeate the atmosphere with thanksgiving and forget about yourself. Sing praises to Me, and joy will follow. Turn your frustration over to Me and reach out to others.

By giving yourself away, you receive. A comforting hug in the midst of a tragedy says, "I care." A smile can brighten the day of someone who is sad. When you put your arm around a shoulder of a hurting person, it's like wrapping them up in a warm, cozy blanket on a cold winter day. Show compassion, mercy, and love, and you will become more and more like Me in your daily life.

"Then you will know the truth, and the truth will set you free."
John 8:32

Into the Deep

My Jesus,

I'm fearful of stepping out in faith. I hesitate to risk the possibility of failure. Show me what to do.

My child,

Don't cling to the security of the shore. Venture out into the deep with Me where people are drowning. Many are drowning in seas of regret over past mistakes. They have no hope; they see no future. Some are in such deep despair and dark depression; they can barely keep their heads above the water. They foolishly cling to the false hope the world offers, and the world mocks them. They don't realize that as quickly as the tide of acceptance comes in, the tide of condemnation goes out, carrying them with it. They are sinking.

Rescue them. Offer them the life preserver of My love. Tell them that just as I reached out to Peter when he was sinking, I am reaching out to them today. Be My advocate. Be My voice. Assure them they are not condemned. They are forgiven. I offer hope and unconditional love, and I am the only way to safety. There is a troubled world waiting.

Remember, I am with you always, and My love endures forever.

"This is the message you have heard from the beginning: We should love one another."
1 John 3:11 (NLT)

Love Is of God

My Jesus,

How I love You!

My child,

Love Me by loving others. Go about your day looking for others to love. Hurting people are everywhere.

Imagine you have a basket full of flowers you hand out as you journey through life. Sometimes that flower is a smile that brightens a sad person's life. Sometimes it's a kind word spoken at the right moment that lifts another out of the pit of despair.

Listen closely for My voice. I am always available. Stay in close contact with Me, and I will send others to you. You need My wisdom to help them. Remember, in Me; you are strong. You are an overcomer.

Let us go forward together.

"For we walk by faith, not by sight."
2 Corinthians 5:7

Do Your Part

My Jesus,

Nothing is working. I don't know where to turn. I try one thing I think is the right thing, and the door gets slammed in my face. This is so frustrating. I don't know what to do. I am so disheartened! I want to give up.

My child,

Have you ever considered I might be closing those doors? I only want the best for you, and sometimes that means saying, "No."

When My servant, Paul, tried to enter Asia and then, later on, Bithynia, to preach, My Holy Spirit would not allow it. I didn't tell him why; he only knew he wasn't to go there. Paul followed My leading and obeyed and went another direction, much like a child should obey when a loving parent says "no," knowing the parent can see dangers the child is not aware of.

When you find yourself flustered, sit quietly and refocus on Me and trust. Keep going. Keep moving forward. Put one foot in front of the others and walk by faith. Follow your dream. See these rejections as stepping stones on your way to My ultimate purpose for you.

"The life of mortals is like grass, they flourish like a flower of the field; the wind blows over it and it is gone, and its place remembers it no more."
Psalm 103:15–16

Number Your Days

My Jesus,

I am weak, but I want to be used by You. What can I do? What can I say? My desire is to follow You closely and bring You joy.

My child,

Speak softly to My people, telling them their sins are forgiven. So many are beaten down, straining as they try to carry the burden of their sins on their shoulders as they transverse through life. This is not My will. Comfort and encourage them and tell them how much I long for them as a mother longs for her wayward child. Tell them to lift up their eyes to behold the heavens and see the night sky and try to count the stars, and then try comprehending My majesty.

To all, I say, your life is in My hands. Make the most of your days. You are like a wildflower, beautiful as it sways in the breeze. Soon that same breeze becomes a wind that blows over it, and it is gone. It is remembered no more. So, I say to you, do not miss one opportunity to do good for you do not know what tomorrow will bring. Live for today.

I give wisdom for each situation, and I desire all to come to Me. Do not fear you are incapable. Look to Me; I am more than capable. Don't beat yourself up dwelling on what might have been or what you should have said and didn't. Be a messenger for My Spirit, leave the outcome to Me, and press on.

I alone will give you the strength you need. Praise Me for all I have done. I am your Father, and My love is unending and eternal.

A Trusting Heart

"Come to me, all you who are weary and burdened, and I will give you rest. Take my yoke upon you and learn from me, for I am gentle and humble in heart, and you will find rest for your souls."
Matthew 11:28–29

Burden So Heavy

My Jesus,

I feel incredibly sad and broken. This is too great a burden for me. I'm powerless and feel like I'm going to break down any second. I am not sleeping and barely functioning. Don't hide from me. I am groaning and weeping into my pillow.

My child,

I have not abandoned you; I feel the depths of your pain. I love you, and I will sustain you. Come out of the darkness of despair and trust Me. Trust me during heartache. Trust me when you don't understand. You will get through this. Don't miss what's ahead because you're stuck in what might have been. You are mourning the loss of the dreams you had. Sit with Me a while, and don't give up.

Come close to Me. I am here with you so you won't be there alone. Emerge from the fog of unbelief and trust Me. Don't give up. It's not over; press on holding My hand as we go.

"To all who mourn in Israel He will give: beauty for ashes; joy instead of mourning; praise instead of heaviness. For God has planted them like strong and graceful oaks for His own glory."
Isaiah 61:3 (TLB)

Feel My Arms around You

My Jesus,

I need You, Lord, but You feel so far away. I am filled with sorrow.

My child,

I am here, where I've always been, but you are unaware of My nearness because you are preoccupied with other things. Come back to Me, come often. Seek a fresh anointing and be filled with My Spirit.

Don't let the cares of this world rob you of the joy and peace that belongs to you. Step into the future with Me. Seek Me more diligently than you ever have. Seek My presence, not My gifts. Sit in solitude, raise your empty cup, and I will fill it to overflowing with My gifts. When you are anxious, I will give you peace. When you are lonely, I will be your companion. When you are sad and discouraged, I will lift your head.

I have need of you just as you have need of Me. My desire is to draw you close and live in constant fellowship with you. What glory lies ahead—reach for it by faith, knowing I am with you always. Tomorrow is another day. Be at peace.

"In addition to all this, take up the shield of faith, with which you can extinguish all the flaming arrows of the evil one. Take the helmet of salvation and the sword of the Spirit, which is the word of God."
Ephesians 6:16–17

Dark Places

My Jesus,

It's so dark in here, in this place. I'm in so much pain; I don't know what to do. I'm spiraling headfirst down a deep hole, and I can't stop myself.

My child,

I feel your anguish, and I am here, right beside you. There is a solution to your pain. When the days are dark and dreary, and there seems to be no way out, let the spirit of praise rise up within you.

Praise is like a vapor going through the atmosphere that parts the dark clouds and reveals the sunlight. When situations seem hopeless, and you feel you can't go on, praise Me. Recall the many times I brought you through. Don't dwell on the bad; focus on My goodness and power to bring you to victory. Resist the enemy at every turn. You are equipped with My Word.

Learn to use My Word as a sword. Stay alert, persevere, and be prepared. Speak My Word out loud into your situation. The more you speak it, the more you hear it and build your faith. For as it is written, faith comes by hearing and hearing by the Word of God.

I don't expect you to fight this battle on your own. You can't. Seek out someone to pray with you, for there is power in agreement. There is comfort when another comes alongside a person. Through that person, feel Me putting My arms around you and be at peace. Know that I care so deeply for you, and through Me you are more than a conqueror, because I love you. (Romans 8:31).

"But the LORD said to Samuel, 'Do not consider his appearance or his height, for I have rejected him. The LORD does not look at the things people look at. People look at the outward appearance, but the LORD looks at the heart.'"
1 Samuel 16:7

Outward Appearances

My Jesus,

I see so many who are rejecting you. Some mock, some ridicule, and some just don't care. It makes me sad and mad, all at the same time. I don't understand how some people can behave so badly and say such hurtful things.

My child,

Look beyond what you're seeing. A person is so much more than outward appearances. Pull the curtains back and see what has been hidden. Open your spiritual eyes—hurting people are all around you. Sometimes these outward mannerisms are masking the hurt that's within.

See yourself closing the door, no, slamming the door on what you think you know. People need what you have. Don't let preconceived ideas or prejudice keep you from sharing. Many have been wounded in ways you don't know. Put your feelings aside; let love be your guide, and leave the rest to Me.

Remember, it's not about you.

"It is God who arms me with strength and keeps my way secure."
Psalm 18:32

Guidance of the Holy Spirit

My Jesus,

I am consumed with anxiety and worry. Where will I go; what will I do? I have great ideas and good intentions. If You're holding me, why does it hurt so bad? I wait on You, Lord. I wait with anticipation and hope, with hands lifted high in praise.

My child,

Be assured that I am holding you. Hear My words. They will light the path in front of you.

So, I say to you, get up and get moving. Don't say, "I have prayed, Jesus will provide," and then do nothing. Don't sit around and wait for that knock on the door or for that special phone call. And don't waste your time feeling sorry for yourself. Do all that you can do and leave the rest to Me. Test everything.

We are on a journey. Let go of your plans and follow Me. My Holy Spirit will be your guide. Walk with Me, step-by-step, as we encounter the newness that awaits you. If the Israelites hadn't stepped into the Red Sea, they would never have gotten to the Promised Land.

"Finally, be strong in the Lord and in his mighty power. Put on the full armor of God, so that you can take your stand against the devil's schemes."
Ephesians 6:10–11

The Battle Is Yours

My Jesus,

I am weary and drained from this battle. Will it never end? I have prayed and prayed, and still, I see nothing. If anything, it's worse. Why don't You do something? What else can I do?

My child,

I will never, ever violate a person's free will. What can you do, you ask? You can continue to pray and pray without ceasing because eternity is at stake. Remember, you are in a war, a spiritual war with spiritual forces of evil. Look to Me for your strength and do not become weary.

A harvest is coming if you do not give up. You are not helpless or without resources. I've provided you with the weapons you need. Be resolute and willing to stand. A soldier doesn't have the option to leave the conflict when it gets hard. Do not abandon your post! You are in the Lord's army

"Immediately Jesus reached out His hand and caught him. 'You of little faith,' He said, 'why did you doubt?'"
Matthew 14:31

Stepping Stones

My Jesus,

This news was so unexpected. I am so unprepared, and I feel so vulnerable. I need You now more than I ever have. Help me, Jesus. I fall into Your arms.

My child,

This life is filled with hardships and sorrow; this is the human condition, and no one escapes it. But I say to you, My child, these afflictions are but stepping stones on the route to your final destination. Imagine a stream filled with rocks that make a pathway to the other side. You scale the stream, keeping one foot on the stone while reaching for the next one, and before you know it, you're on the other side, one step at a time.

As difficult as it may be, remember I am with you. Go slowly. We will walk together, navigating through the rapids of life. Don't try to skip any step; you might lose your way, slip, and fall. As I beckoned Peter to focus on Me when he was walking on the water, I am beckoning you to stay focused on Me. Only when Peter looked at his circumstances and took his eyes off Me, did he begin to sink.

I am not asking you to ignore the problem; do all you can and then leave the rest to Me. Just as I was there for Peter, I will always be there for you.

"I call out to the LORD, and he answers me from his holy mountain."
Psalm 3:4

Look Up

My Jesus,

The sky is dark and dreary today, and rain clouds are forming. It's threatening to pour. As water weighs down the clouds, I am weighed down with despair and hopelessness. These burdens drape over me like a heavy blanket, too heavy to carry. I am worn out from crying. Where are you, God?

My child,

The sun is still there, even though the dark clouds and the circumstances coming against you hide it. Allow Me to dry your tears and lift your head. Hear Me whisper words of comfort to you. I will never leave you. Reach out and touch Me. Trust Me, and I will lead you.

When things around you are falling apart, don't run from Me, run to Me. Do not be afraid. Remember, all I've done before and look to the future. I am moving you in a new direction. Look up!

"'Lord, if it's You,' Peter replied, 'tell me to come to You on the water.' 'Come,' He said."
Matthew 14:28–29

Step out of the Boat

My Jesus,

The future is unknown, and I'm frightened.

My child,

I am calling you to greater heights than you have ever been. I'm calling you to step out of your boat onto the waters of uncertainty. Your boat is your place of security. It may be your home, your children, your job, or your church. It may be an addiction you're clinging to. You've grown comfortable in your misery and fear letting go. You can remain there if you want, but you risk becoming like a rocking chair, back and forth, back and forth, going nowhere.

I am calling you to come up higher. When I challenged Peter to walk with Me on the water, it was dark and stormy, and the boat was far from shore, far from security. It was being buffeted by relentless seas. It was the hour just before dawn, the darkest hour when I bid him to come. I come to you too, in your darkest hour, and bid you to come, so come.

Quiet your mind and hear Me say to you, as I said to the disciples, "don't be afraid, I am here." Don't focus on the darkness; don't focus on the storm, but focus on Me. Stretch out your arm, take My hand,

and we will begin the journey. I will set you on a new path, and we will walk together on the waters.

*"Hear, O LORD, and have mercy on me;
LORD, be my helper!"
Psalm 30:10 (NKJV)*

The Lonely Path

My Jesus,

I hear so many voices, all with differing opinions. I don't know which way to go, where to turn. I'm so confused. Give me the grace to always be attuned to Your voice. Speak to me as I seek solitude with You—the only way to drown out the noise of the world.

My child,

Come to the garden and sit with Me awhile. Listen to the whispers of nature and be refreshed. Do you not hear the rustling of the wind through the trees? You can't see the wind just as you can't see Me, but it's there. Let that serve as a reminder that I am here, and I am with you.

Rest with Me a while and be comforted. I will be your peace and strength, and I will bring you through. Put your trust in Me and walk by faith, not by sight. Never doubt My love for you. My arms are around you, holding you tightly and shielding you from collapse. You are Mine, and My love for you is without end.

"'For Your sake we face death all day long; we are considered as
sheep to be slaughtered.'
No, in all these things we are more than conquerors through him
who loved us."
Romans 8:36–37

More Than a Conqueror

My Jesus,

How can I be more than a conqueror? I am struggling to win this battle. Sometimes, I think it will overtake me and swallow me up! It's hard for me to believe You even care, let alone love me. Help my unbelief!

My child,

You are in this battle, but remember, you are not alone. I am by your side. You conquer when you win your battle. But you are more than a conqueror when you rely on Me alone.

Only I know the end from the beginning. It looked to the world like Jesus lost His battle when He died on the cross. Three days later, He rose, conquered death, and the world was forever changed. He was more than a conqueror!

When your circumstances look hopeless, think on these things and be encouraged. Raise your head high and say, "Nothing can ever separate me from the love of God that is in Christ Jesus, our Lord!" (See Romans 8:38–39).

"The rain came down, the streams rose, and the winds blew and beat against that house; yet it did not fall, because it had its foundation on the rock."
Matthew 7:25

The Seed

My Jesus,

I don't want to fear. I don't want to be afraid, but it is so hard when I don't understand all that is going on around me. Why is this happening? When will it stop?

My child,

Be still, My child, and listen as I speak these truths to you. When a seed is planted in the ground, the rain comes and helps the seed to grow. The harder the rain falls, the deeper the seed goes, and roots form. The roots are hidden deep beneath the earth, where they grow in secret.

So it is with you. When adversity comes, like a fierce, raging storm, beating at you relentlessly and attempting to blow you off course, stand strong! Realize the harder the wind blows, the deeper your roots will go. When the storm finally settles, that seed will have grown and will eventually become a majestic oak tree, standing great and tall, able to resist the fiercest of storms when they come again.

"Enter through the narrow gate. For wide is the gate and broad is the road that leads to destruction, and many enter through it. But small is the gate and narrow the road that leads to life, and only a few find it."
Matthew 7:13–14

An Unfamiliar Path

My Jesus,

I am struggling to find my way, and it is so difficult. At times, I feel lost, alone, and scared. I can only make it with Your help.

My child,

Walk silently beside me; I have chosen this path, so do not be surprised it is a foreign way to you, a way you would not have chosen. Follow closely until I show you the next step. Though the way is strewn with rocks and deep crevices, remember I am walking with you, and I know the way. I may not lift you above and over the hard places, but I will be with you. We will go forward together.

I am taking you along a long, narrow, steep, and sometimes solitary road. Only then will you understand how to trust Me in all circumstances. How would you learn if I gave you free rein to go your own way? I am making you strong and courageous, an example for the weak.

Stay close to Me, and I will become a place of peace and comfort for you as we travel this road together.

Lost Hope

My Jesus,

I know I must walk this difficult path; there is no way out, but through. I am devastated. I sit alone; everyone has left me. If you leave me, Lord, I don't know what I'll do. You are my only hope.

My child,

There was a time when I, too, was in anguish. I was in the garden of Gethsemane, alone. I was in agony. It looked like all hope was lost. Everyone had left Me. On the cross, I cried out to My Father, asking why even He had abandoned Me. There was only silence. All the time, there was a greater plan, a much greater plan being worked out secretly. No one ever could have imagined.

I implore you to hold on. A new day is dawning. Victory will come. Close the door on the past, and walk with Me into the future. Walk with Me into a new normal. Let's anticipate the wonders waiting just around the corner in the next phase of your life.

Remember, I am with you, and I will never leave you.

"This is the day the LORD has made. We will rejoice and be glad in it."
Psalm 118:24 (NLT)

Constant Companion

My Jesus,

Thank You for another day. No matter what it may bring, I pray You will be with me.

My child,

I am with you, as I always have been and always will be. I hold eternity in My hands. As you walk through this life, picture Me right next to you. Sometimes, I gently hold you back from a peril that lies ahead; sometimes, I urge you forward into uncharted territory. Wherever you go, I am already there. You are never alone.

Practice being aware of My presence. See My beauty in the fragrant flowers of spring and the small delicate rosebuds of summer. See My strength in the majestic trees of the forest as they reach to heaven. Feel My tenderness when you cradle a newborn baby in your arms. These are My gifts to you, reminders of My love. Let them inspire your hope and fill you with courage and confidence.

Go forward. Cast all your cares on Me, and I will sustain you.

"Then Jesus said to His disciples, 'Whoever wants to be my disciple must deny themselves and take up their cross and follow me.'"
Matthew 16:24

Arise

My Jesus,

Where are You? This weight is too heavy; the hardship is too much. I can't bear the load any longer.

My child,

Don't be surprised by the distress you are experiencing. Have I not told you that in this world you will have tribulation? In the midst of your pain, suffering, and disappointment, offer Me a sacrifice of praise. Focus on Me and watch as your cares fade into the distance. Let them become a mist, a praise offering to Me. As I lift your burdens from you, you are no longer encumbered by the cares of this world. Only then are you free to minister to others I send your way.

You must be free to do My work. My blood made you clean and free. You are no longer a slave in this world. However, there is an enemy who is the master of evil. He is ever-present, watching for an opening into your life.

Do not allow unforeseen circumstances to weigh you down. You must rise, not in your own strength, but in Mine. It was never My intention that you should carry heavy burdens. The only burden you are to carry is the cross you use to crucify the flesh—the selfish desires that keep you from becoming all that I mean for you to be. Know you are capable, you are loved and together we are victorious!

"You are my hiding place and my shield; I hope in Your Word."
Psalm 119:114 (NRSV)

Noah

My Jesus,

I'm overwhelmed! I don't know what to do! Please help me.

My child,

When the storms of life come—and they will—think of Noah. He was saved from the storm because he was hidden away in the ark. He could hear the winds blowing and the storm raging while the ark rocked violently on the sea. He had no assurance of safety other than My Word.

He couldn't see the whole picture. How could he foresee the plans I had for him? I only asked him to obey when he didn't have all the answers and didn't understand.

Many times you don't see the big picture. These are the times you must trust and rely on Me. Remember; My love dictates everything I do. Allow Me to be your refuge. I hide you away from dangers all around you, many you are not even aware of.

I am molding you into My image. I am fashioning a one-of-a-kind masterpiece. Be still, my child. Many are the plans I have for you.

Wait, and see.

"Trust in the LORD with all your heart and lean not on your own understanding."
Proverbs 3:5

Safe in My Care

My Jesus,

You have said to trust You. How do I do that when there is so much destruction all around?

My child,

I am calling you to a life of total reliance on Me. Just as a little child takes her father's hand as they cross the street, so you must put your hand in Mine as we walk through this life together. Be careful not to let go, even for a second.

This world is full of danger, heartache, disappointment, and pain. How I wish it was not so. Many things are out of your control. When you don't understand and nothing makes sense, that is when you must grasp My hand even more tightly and trust Me.

Trust My heart, trust My goodness, and trust My love. I will strengthen and help you. Know that I am working behind the scenes, where you do not see. I am going to do a new thing. I will make a way through the chaos.

So, come to Me, My child, My dear one. Pour your heart out to Me and cry. Lean only on Me. Know that in Me, you are strong, and you will go confidently into the future, with Me as your guide.

"Through Jesus, therefore, let us continually offer to God a sacrifice of praise — the fruit of lips that openly profess His name."
Hebrews 13:15

Unanswered Questions

My Jesus,

Please help me get through this day and let go of the past. Why is it so difficult? I don't understand so many things, and I have many unanswered questions. Things happen that make no sense. I feel as though my faith is failing. Help me, Jesus.

My child,

Faith simply believes when you do not see. It is believing in the One who fashioned the world out of nothing, hung the stars in the sky, and gave you life. Is there anything too hard for Me?

Put aside your questions and come to Me. Pour your heart out and allow Me to comfort you. Sit quietly in My presence as I wipe away your tears.

Someday you will minister to others, but not now. Drop your unanswered prayers at My feet. Do not allow yourself to become anxious and confused. Instead, offer Me a sacrifice of praise and thanksgiving. Don't become upset by what you don't understand. Focus only on My love for you.

This is a lonely path you walk, but you are not walking it alone. I am leading you. Stay close to me.

"The LORD is my strength and my shield; my heart trusts in Him, and He helps me. My heart leaps for joy and with my song I praise Him."
Psalm 28:7

Where Are You, Lord?

Oh, Jesus,

I am overwhelmed and devastated. Nothing is turning out as I had planned. I'm feeling empty inside, and so sad and weary. I want to believe things will be normal again, but they might not be. I'm scared and lonely. Help me rely on You and have faith.

My precious child,

Do not fear. Lean on Me when your world is spinning out of control. I have a greater plan that you do not see. I am right here, where I've always been, and My grace is enough. I am not mad at you because you question Me.

Do you imagine that Ruth questioned the plan I had for her? Her world was turned upside down by circumstances out of her control. She was a widow who also lost a brother-in-law and father-in-law. She had to leave her home and choose not to abandon her mother-in-law but to accompany her to a land she didn't know.

Ruth kept on doing the right thing in the midst of uncertainty. She could never have imagined that someday she would be the great-grandmother to King David.

Be brave, don't give up. Expect great things. Look forward with eyes of faith.

"I have told you these things, so that in Me you may have peace. In this world you will have trouble. But, take heart! I have overcome the world."
John 16:33 (NIV)

Spirit of Fear

My Jesus,

I am uneasy and overcome with anxiety. My world seems to be falling apart, and I am powerless. I don't want to fall into despair.

My child,

A spirit of fear and anxiety has overtaken some of My children. There are many things in the world you cannot control. Be concerned with the things in your power to change.

The secret to victory over those things that so easily frustrate you is a life lived close to me. I am but a breath away, and no weapon formed against you will prosper (Isaiah 54:17). The key to that knowledge is a life of prayer. I have promised if you draw near to Me, I will draw near to you. I will comfort you and raise you above your circumstances. Make your daily prayer a priority.

I am building a strong army, and I need well-equipped and disciplined soldiers. You have been equipped with My Word; now, it's up to you to manifest the discipline! I stand ready to help you, but the enemy is also ready to discourage you. He has no power over you other than what you give him.

So rise up! Resolve this day to pray and read My Word. Watch how you grow, watch how you change, and watch how you become the person you were always meant to be. Leave the failures of the past in the past, and begin anew this day.

"I am the way and the truth and the life. No one comes to the Father except through Me."
John 14:6

Perilous Times

My Jesus,

I don't know what tomorrow may bring, and I'm frightened. Help me trust You and have faith. Show me what I should do.

My child,

You are living in perilous times. Don't trouble yourself trying to figure out the future. I shield it from you with mercy. It is enough for you to be concerned with this present day. The days are racing to an end, and still so many need to know Me as I really am.

Many see Me as an angry taskmaster waiting for them to mess up, so I can punish them. They are burdened with feelings of guilt and condemnation that keep them from Me. They have no hope, but I offer hope. They need the truth. I am the truth. They need to be loved. I am longing to love and forgive them. I do not harbor anger for those who have done wrong. I am filled with tender mercy and compassion, and My arms are outstretched, always open.

This is My assignment for you: Be more aware of those around you. Keep your spiritual eyes and ears open. Be merciful to those who doubt. Show love and kindness to those who are lost. Look for ways to be a blessing. Share the hope that you have in Me. Share your love, share your story, and share your life. You are My ambassador on earth. I am seeking lost souls through you.

Comfort of the Holy Spirit

"Consider it pure joy, my brothers and sisters, whenever you face trials of many kinds, because you know that the testing of your faith produces perseverance."
James 1:2–3

The Easy Way

My Jesus,

There has got to be an easier way. Why is it so difficult? I thought this would be something more manageable, less burdensome to navigate. I want to give up.

My child,

Don't be tempted to take the easy, painless way. Follow the path I set before you. Think of Abraham. When I called him, I didn't tell him where he was going. He moved in faith, following the route I set before him. Many tests were along the path, there had to be, but I was always with him. He passed the tests and became a great and powerful nation.

I'm here for you, and I see your struggles you may not understand now, and you may never understand. This is a growing time. You must trust Me. I do not change. I am the same now as I was then. This is a stretching time for you. This is how your faith will grow. Look to Me for wisdom. I will be right with you while you're walking through this trial.

"I am worn out from my groaning. All night long I flood my bed with weeping and drench my couch with tears. My eyes grow weak with sorrow; they fail because of all my foes."
Psalm 6:6–7

It's Raining

My Jesus,

It's raining in my heart. My pillow is stained with tears. I can't believe this has happened. I don't understand. Where are You, Lord? I am discouraged and so angry, but I'm looking to You for strength. I know You hear my cries. Answer quickly, I pray. I am slipping under the waves, the waves of sorrow, anger, and unforgiveness.

My child,

Come to Me and do not fear. In your pain, you question everything, even My love for you. It's hard to see beyond your heartache. But know this, I am right beside you, and I will never leave you or forsake you.

What has been done is done and needs to be left in the past. Don't hold onto unforgiveness or harbor unkind thoughts or thoughts of revenge. They will destroy you. Think of what is afflicting you now and put Me in the picture.

Imagine Me walking with you, going before you, and clearing the way. Let go and leave the consequences to Me.

"Forgetting what is behind and straining toward what is ahead, I press on toward the goal to win the prize for which God has called me heavenward in Christ Jesus."
Philippians 3:13–14

Kindness of God

My Jesus,

My heart is broken because of what I've done. You trusted me, and I failed You. I cannot forgive myself. This guilt is too much to bear.

My child,

Imagine yourself holding a baby bird you rescued from the dangers in the world. She has grown and flourished, but there comes a time to release her back into the unknown. You want to protect her from all the snares that could trap her, but if you did, she wouldn't be free. So, you let her go. That's how I feel about you. I rescued you from the entrapments of humanity. I freed you, taught you, cared for you, and loved you, and then it was time to release you back into the world.

The difference between the bird and you is that once you release the bird, she is gone from your sight. You couldn't be with her if you wanted to. She has flown into the unknown, and she has only herself to rely on.

Not so with you. I am always with you to comfort, forgive, and love. The enemy is a deceiver—accusing, condemning, lying, and out to kill. He will shatter your dreams if you let him. You will grow to hear My voice more and more clearly as you renew your mind with My words of love and encouragement. You will get to know what My perfect will is, and you will be able to withstand the lies of the enemy.

Now, it's time to press on. Don't waste another minute lamenting over what was done; receive My forgiveness and press on. Reach for all that lies ahead. A lost world is waiting.

"Going a little farther, he fell with his face to the ground and prayed, 'My Father, if it is possible, may this cup be taken from Me. Yet not as I will, but as You will.'"
Matthew 26:39

I'm Hurting

My Jesus,

I'm swirling in the sea of my emotions. I can't believe this is happening. I have no control. I know my faith is being strengthened, but I don't want this. Isn't there any other way? I'm like a tiny boat drifting in a vast ocean, lost and abandoned.

My child,

In preparing Him for what I knew was to come, I led Jesus to the desert. It was out of love that I compelled Him to the wilderness. He needed to know He could conquer and withstand the pressure before Him.

What desert are you in now? Is your loyalty, your faith, or your patience being tested? Are you able to remain strong in the midst of adversity? The enemy lies waiting to trip you up and spoil the plans I have for you. Be alert, wise to his devices. Stop him at every turn. Remember, My Word is your sword.

Stay close to Me, enclosed in by My protection, covered with My blood and watch as the enemy flees.

"When Jesus came by, he looked up at Zacchaeus and called him by name! 'Zacchaeus!' He said. 'Quick! Come down! For I am going to be a guest in your home today!'"
Luke 19:5 (TLB)

Rejected

My Jesus,

I fall into your arms—I am exhausted from trying and long for Your comfort. Everywhere I go, people overlook and reject me. I feel isolated and abandoned. I don't want to try anymore. What's the use?

My child,

I, too know the heartache of rejection. Where were My friends at My greatest hour of need? I hung on the cross, alone.

I am here for you, as I always have been. When you are feeling unwanted, overlooked, and neglected, stop, and think of David. He was alone, tending to the sheep. He wasn't even considered when Samuel came to Jesse's house looking for the future king. No one saw him in that lonely field, but I did.

And think of Zacchaeus—he had no friends and those who knew him rejected him. He was so small he had to climb a tree so that he could see Me. I saw him just as I see you. I had great plans for these men who no one saw.

Your path may be lonely at times, but I say to you, keep doing what you're doing; don't give up. I am watching, and at the right time, I will lift you.

"And if, as my representatives, you give even a cup of cold water to a little child, you will surely be rewarded."
Matthew 10:42 (TLB)

Lord, I'm Weary!

My Jesus,

I don't think I can go on another day! The tasks are too many! Forgive me for not doing more for You. I want to do great things for You.

My child,

I hear your prayer, and I see how tirelessly you work. Never think you wasted your days because you're not doing "great" things for me. You might think that because you're not preaching, leading crowded revival meetings, writing timeless hymns that will be sung throughout the ages, or singing songs that bring tears to the eyes of the listeners, you're not doing anything for Me.

You spend your days tirelessly caring for My little ones unable to care for themselves. It may be a baby, a child, or an invalid. As you care for them, you are representing Me. Don't measure by the world's standards. I am watching everything, and this is truly a "great" thing.

Always remember, you are not alone; I see all that you do, and I honor you. Did I not say that if you so much as gave a cup of cold water to one of these little ones, you are doing it for Me?

Know that I am so very proud of you, and I am not looking for the next superstar. I am looking for a heart devoted to Me. You can rest in whatever your task is for the day. Ask Me to bless your effort, and I will.

"Finally, brothers and sisters, whatever is true, whatever is noble, whatever is right, whatever is pure, whatever is lovely, whatever is admirable—if anything is excellent or praiseworthy—think about such things."
Philippians 4:8

Buried Deep

My Jesus,

I am drowning in the shame of past sins. I know I'm forgiven, but my mind keeps tormenting me with the things I've done. I am distraught!

My child,

Ask yourself if you are believing a lie? If you know you're forgiven, why are you allowing the enemy to persecute you? Consider what you are thinking about.

Your thoughts are more powerful than you know, and they direct your life. Your thoughts become the words you speak. If you focus on the wrong thing, soon those words become a reality—a reality you don't want. Soon you are reliving all the things you have done wrong and tormenting yourself for sins that have been forgiven and should have been buried long ago. Life keeps moving on, but you remain stuck in a prison of your own making.

Thoughts are powerful. If you think for too long about how another person hurt you, it won't be long before you're figuring out how you can hurt that person rather than forgive them. Pretty soon, you're plotting revenge instead of forgiveness, and the enemy has won. Holding on to unforgiveness only harms you.

Why else would I tell you to guard your heart and fix your thoughts on things that are true, honorable, and right? My final instructions to the Philippian church was about their thoughts. I told them to think only good thoughts so that My peace would settle on them.

You are forgiven, My child. See yourself burying your past sins, see them buried deep, and see yourself walking on the ground they lie beneath. I have placed all things under your feet—I am merciful. Leave the past in the past and go forward free. A new day is dawning.

"I waited patiently for the LORD; he turned to me and heard my cry."
Psalm 40:1 (NIV)

The Waiting Room

My Jesus,

Hear my cry, my heart. Nothing is going as I thought it would, as I had planned and prayed for. I am drowning in the weight of my thoughts. Rescue me before I sink under the waves of oppression and fear. I am like a man treading water in rough seas, and I can barely hold on. I am numb. Come to me soon. Where else can I go?

My child,

I am with you. Slow down, come into My presence if only for a few minutes, and fix your thoughts on Me.

Rest in my arms as I speak peace to you. Allow Me to quiet your racing mind. Don't exchange your peace and joy for hopelessness and despair. Wait on Me and renew your strength. Many lessons can only be learned in the waiting room of life. Do not be afraid. I am holding you.

"Be still and know that I am God; I will be exalted among the nations, I will be exalted in the earth."
Psalm 46:10

Be Still

My Jesus,

During the chaos, I call to You. Please quiet my racing mind.

My child,

When your world is falling apart, turn to Me. Pause with Me a while and be still. Listen to the silence of your heart; I am speaking peace to you. When you're losing all hope and paralyzed with fear, come to Me with praise, thanksgiving, and worship Me. Remember things I did in the past, rejoice, and be encouraged. Trust Me to deliver you and lead you forward.

If you've fallen, look up. Picture Me reaching down to lift you and bring you close to My heart. Imagine you're cold and I wrap you in a warm blanket. Rest quietly in My arms, and let Me hold you securely. You have no need to fear. I will comfort you and give you a sweet sleep.

I desire for you to be so sure of My love that when you call on Me, you know I will be there to bring you out of your distress. Come into My presence, quiet your racing mind, and be still before Me. I will show you great and mighty things.

"May these words of my mouth and this meditation of my heart be pleasing in your sight, LORD, my Rock and my Redeemer."
Psalm 19:14

Words

My Jesus,

I am Your minister. What can I do for You?

My child,

See yourself as My ambassador, on assignment, searching daily for the downtrodden, the forgotten, the lonely, and the dejected. One word from you, spoken with love, can lift a person out of their misery, set them on a different path to begin their life anew. Become a dispenser of goodness, blessing people wherever you go.

Imagine yourself carrying a beautiful bouquet, and wherever you go, you give out a blossom. Maybe it's a blossom of a smile or a kind word.

There is power in every word you speak—power to tear down, build up, inspire, or power to depress. Words can encourage a dream, or they can demolish hope when thoughtlessly spoken. What words are you speaking to yourself or others?

Choose your words carefully. Be mindful of the force they are. Above all My creations, only you were made with the capacity to inspire others to greatness with your words. It is an awesome responsibility. Do not take it lightly.

"That person is like a tree planted by streams of water, which yields its fruit in season and whose leaf does not wither—whatever they do prospers."
Psalm 1:3

Rest for the Weary

My Jesus,

I am discouraged, confused, and I don't understand. I didn't see this coming, and now I feel I've been forgotten, abandoned, and left alone. My mind is spinning out of control. This is so unfair!

My precious child,

How often have My children been too busy to spend time with Me after they said they would? They tell Me they'll come tomorrow when it's a better time, but they become preoccupied with other things and don't come. They won't enjoy the gifts I'm longing to give them—gifts I so carefully prepared.

As you share My distress, you are becoming more like Me. My goal is that you become like a tree planted by still water. Quietly, silently in the depths of the earth, that tree grows, producing strong branches that will bring forth leaves that someday provide shade for those hurting and need comfort and rest.

"Let the morning bring me word of Your unfailing love, for I have put my trust in you. Show me the way I should go, for to You I entrust my life."
Psalm 143:8

Let Me Love You

My Jesus,

My thoughts weigh heavily on my mind. I am distraught, and I want to run away! Where can I escape and find rest? Where can I go? My enemies surround me!

My child,

Don't run from Me when you're hurting. Run into My arms. When you are distraught, I will sustain you and give you rest. You only need to trust Me. Come to Me and let Me love you.

Visualize a child, walking on an unsafe path. Would not her earthly mother lift her over the danger? In the same way, imagine Me lifting you above your circumstances just as I lifted Peter out of the waters when he was sinking.

Rest in My arms, fall asleep, and let Me love you. Imagine Me restoring your broken heart—a heart shattered into a million pieces. Allow Me to repair it shard by shard.

Your tragedy can become your mission. You will be able to reach out to others whose hearts are breaking and need to be comforted. You will reach out in a way no one else can. You can't see it now, but soon you will have hope to share with humanity.

Press on. Just keep moving, one foot in front of the other, secure in My love. You are never alone!

"As a mother comforts her child, so I will comfort you; and you will be comforted over Jerusalem."
Isaiah 66:13

The Way of Peace

My Jesus,

I don't know where to go or what to do. The future is uncertain, and I'm so scared of what might lie ahead of me. I hear so many bad reports. Be near me, Jesus, I pray.

My child,

Do not give in to the spirit of fear. When you hear something and take it in, you meditate on it, and before you know it, you're thinking the worst. This is not My way. My way is the way of peace and love. Remember, I am always with you, and I will never leave you. You may feel alone, but My hand is upon you.

Let your worry melt into prayer and let praise fill your lips. Change your thinking, refocus, and meditate on the best—My best— not the worst. Then watch as I displace worry and fear. Picture Me holding you, comforting you as a mother comforts her child.

Gather your concerns, place them in My hands, and leave them with Me. You won't be relieved of the burden if you take them back. When your thoughts are contrary to My Word, you open yourself up to the enemy. Only you can oppose My peace.

"He gives strength to the weary and increases the power of the weak."
Isaiah 40:29

Draw Near to Me

My Jesus,

Why is it so painful? When will the agony stop? I'm unable to think clearly, and I'm so confused. I feel so helpless.

My child,

Picture Me holding you now, speaking words of comfort and drying your tears. When the sun is shining and the day is beautiful, it is easy to trust Me. But on cloudy days, when you don't see the sun, that is when I am testing your faith. I am still there but, hidden for the moment, by the dark, threatening clouds and the circumstances of this life.

Don't base your reality on what you see. Rely only on what you know of Me. I am for you, not against you. I have only love for you. I am found in the anointed pages of Scripture. That is who I am, not what you see or how you feel.

This is not the time to doubt My love or My power to keep you strong. This is the time to draw deep from the spiritual well of strength within you. This is the time to draw closer to Me.

Remember My words to you. My plans for you are unfolding, and My plans are good. There is a future and there is hope. I am holding you in the palm of My hand.

"'I will set out and go back to my father and say to him: Father, I have sinned against heaven and against you. I am no longer worthy to be called your son; make me like one of your hired servants.' So he got up and went to his father. 'But while he was still a long way off, his father saw him and was filled with compassion for him; he ran to his son, threw his arms around him and kissed him.'"
Luke 15:18–20

Forgiveness

My Jesus,

Forgive me, have mercy on me. I can't even come near You; I feel so unworthy. Wash me and cleanse me from my sinfulness. Do not turn away from me, oh Lord.

My child,

Don't run away from Me when you have fallen; run to Me. I have been longing for you to return. I paid for your sins once and for all on the cross. Run quickly into My arms, outstretched and waiting for you. I will refresh, refill, and use you again. The enemy will whisper, "It's too late," but I say to you it is never too late.

It is not My intention that you should bear the heavy burden of your sin. The only thing you are to carry is the cross you use to crucify the flesh—the selfish desires that keep you from becoming all I mean for you to be.

Stand ready, it's a new day. Together we will begin again. Leave the past behind you and imagine a fresh start, a new beginning; that's what I offer you.

Will you accept My gift, or will you continue to beat yourself up? Because I love you so much, I leave the decision to you. As the Scripture says, "Choose you this day whom you will serve" (Joshua 24:15 KJV).

"…Then the angel of God called to Hagar from heaven, and said, "Why are you so troubled Hagar? Do not be afraid.'"
Genesis 21:17 (NLV)

Open My Eyes Lord

My Jesus.

Where can I turn, what can I do? Do You see me? Do You even care? There seems to be no way out; all my hope is gone. I am alone, and I am scared, so very scared.

My child,

Allow Me to comfort you. I see you where you are, and I am here. You are never alone. When you are sad and discouraged, think of my servant Hagar. She was lost and without hope, and she cried out to Me. She found I had not abandoned her. I was with her all along. So, cry out to Me, and remember Hagar in Genesis 21:14, "She wandered on (aimlessly) and lost her way…"

My Jesus,

When I'm walking through my own desert—alone, afraid, lost, and desperate—help me know You are there. Genesis 21:16 "…she raised her voice and wept."

Oh, Jesus, hear my voice, I pray, when I feel so alone, and I am crying. Genesis 21:19 "Then God opened her eyes and she saw a well of water…"

My Jesus, open my spiritual eyes that I might see You and all that You offer me.

"I would hurry to my place of shelter, far from the tempest and storm."
Psalm 55:8

Storms of Life

My Jesus,

Why can't the path I walk on be strewn with flowing green grass and beautiful meadows of fragrant flowers? I would enjoy them immensely, maybe even lie down and rest. Instead, I stumble over hidden rocks. Why do I have to climb steep, treacherous mountains? I struggle with every step on the way up.

Why do unexpected storms arise out of nowhere, raging fiercely against me, all to blow me off the course I travel, a course I thought You ordained? Why is the way so difficult?

My child,

It should not alarm you when you encounter various trials in this life. Picture a lemon used to enhance the flavor of water. First, it is sliced and stuck on the rim of the glass. If it is not removed and squeezed, its full potential will not be realized. Only when it is squeezed and put under pressure, will the flavor come forth and its full capacity is known. It will become all that it was meant to be.

Life on earth is hard, so think it not strange when winds arise to blow you off your path. It is written that in this world you will have tribulation, but it is also written that I have overcome the world (John 16:33).

Be strong, be determined; stay the course. We will get to the other side together!

Psalm 23 (NKJV)

The Lord is my shepherd; I shall not want.

Help me have faith for each day and not worry about tomorrow. I know You care tenderly for me, what more is there to want?

He makes me to lie down in green pastures;

When my days are filled with endless activity, I can easily forget You. When there is suddenly a roadblock in my plans, help me see this as Your gentle reminder to seek You first, Your will, and Your direction. I don't want to whine and moan because my plans didn't turn out the way I planned. I want to want only Your will.

He leads me beside the still water.

Not rushing, turbulent waters but still, peaceful waters reminding me of how much I need that quiet time with You, where I can regain the strength I long for, focusing on You alone.

He restores my soul;

You renew my mind. You revive my will, and soothe my emotions, provide healing where I have been so wounded by this life.

He leads me in the path of righteousness for His name's sake.

You encourage me to always choose to do the right thing, remembering that I represent You wherever I may go.

Yea, though I walk through the valley of the shadow of death, I will fear no evil; for You are with me;

When I am afraid and fear the darkness will overtake me, I will praise You through the pain. You encourage me to keep on walking, step-by-step, out of the shadow, into Your light.

Your rod and Your staff, they comfort me.

A shepherd protects his sheep if they should wander into danger or stumble on their path. You protect me from hidden dangers all around, many I'm not even aware of. With Your staff, You gently guide me back if I should stray from the path of my life. Your love and Your Word comfort me.

You prepare a table for me in the presence of my enemies;

My enemies might be addiction, fear, or sadness, but You have defeated them all! They are under Your feet at the victor's table.

You anoint my head with oil; my cup runs over.

I have the presence of the Holy Spirit with me because You have anointed me. May Your presence overflow into the lives of all who I meet.

Surely goodness and mercy will follow me all the days of my life;

Because of Your great promises and love, I have hope, and I am never alone.

And I will dwell in the house of the LORD forever.

I know when the door closes on today, You will be waiting to walk with me into tomorrow, and I will be with You for all eternity!

Strength for Today

"Whereas you do not know what will happen tomorrow. For what is your life? It is even a vapor that appears for a little time and then vanishes away."
James 4:14 (NKJV)

Life Is a Vapor

My Jesus,

What am I here for? I'm like a shadow constantly moving. I don't want to be a drifter just passing through this life on the way to eternity. I want to bless You, but I don't know how.

My child,

There are many things you can do, so many people to minister to. People are heartbroken and discouraged, just longing for someone to offer a kind word, a shoulder to cry on, and a word of encouragement. As you walk into your future, look for opportunities to lift someone's spirit.

Everyone has a story; take time to listen and care. My fractured world is waiting. There are things that only you can do. No one else has the connections you have, the relationships you have, the talents and the gifts you have, or the personality you have. Don't devalue yourself; you were bought with a price.

Be alert at all times. There is an enemy who does not want the world to know of My love, so he lies, discourages, and tries to keep you down.

When you have lost your momentum, ask yourself, which voice you are listening to. I need you to be a light in the dark world, and I can't use you if you are confused. Stand up to the enemy, resist him, and he will leave. Commit each day to learn more and more of Me. Live your life so near to Me that you will recognize his deceit immediately.

Together we are an unstoppable team. Life is but a vapor that is quickly fading away (James 4:14).

"For everyone who asks receives; the one who seeks finds; and to the one who knocks, the door will be opened."
Matthew 7:8

Turn the Page

My Jesus,

I've lost my vision. I have no dream. I want more of You, but I can't seem to find You. Everything's the same. Save me from this weariness.

My child,

I bid you to come. Shake off apathy. Get out of your spiritual wasteland and go deeper and deeper into spiritual things. Just as someone wades deeper into the water, I want to take you deeper into the water of My Word. Don't settle for a cursory glance—I have so much more to show you. Be persistent and determined. Your vision will return, and you will discover your purpose.

You wouldn't skim a few chapters in a book, put it down, and then think you knew the whole story. Resist thinking that you know it all and becoming vain. Guard against pride.

Keep asking, keep seeking. Keep knocking. I have much to show you, and your joy will return.

There is much to be gained by turning the pages.

"Think about those times of your first love (how different now!) and turn back to Me again and work as you did before."
Revelation 2:5 (TLB)

Slow Down

My Jesus,

I'm feeling downcast and sad, and I don't know why. I need You. I don't know what to do. I feel rushed and pressured. Where am I going wrong?

My child,

Could it be you've let other things divert your attention from Me? It can be easy to overlook and miss Me in the routine of every day.

Don't proceed so quickly that you miss what I have prepared for you. I might be asking you to assist in some way by offering a kind word to lift someone's spirit, being the shoulder someone needs to cry on, or giving a word of encouragement. When you do these things, you are blessed.

As you progress, stop for a moment and absorb the beauty of creation—trees rising majestically to the heavens, a rose garden filling the atmosphere with fragrance, or the distant sound of a dove, welcoming the morning. These are but moments in time easily missed if you are preoccupied and hurry through your day.

Slow down so that I might bless you. There is a danger in taking My gifts for granted. Don't let what was once exciting become mundane. Don't lose your first love. Look for rest stops I provide along the way and slow down. Open your eyes to all I show you. You will once again be amazed and praise will follow.

"Can a mother forget the baby at her breast and have no compassion on the child she has borne? Though she may forget, I will not forget you!"
Isaiah 49:15

Hope

My Jesus,

Have mercy on me. I can't cry anymore—there are no tears left. I'm falling into a ditch of regret, disappointment, and heartache. I can't bear this anymore. If You leave me, where will I go, what will I do? Have you forgotten me?

My child,

Can a mother forget her child? Even if she did, I will not forget you.

You are forgiven and going in a new direction. I say to you to come out, be free. A new adventure awaits. I have anointed you, and My hand sustains you. Remain close to Me and I will shelter you in My shadow and I will be your guard.

Only do not be afraid. Fear opens the door to anxiety, then depression, and finally, hopelessness. But you, my child, are never without hope. Learn to live expectantly. Live by faith.

Gaze at the sunset with a new sense of wonder, take in the ocean's magnificence with new eyes, and gaze at a flower with a sense of awe. These are my gifts to you to lift you above your circumstances. I have only good things planned for you.

Take one step and begin walking into the rest of your life. Leave the past behind. Make a path through the dark forest of doubt and unbelief. I am with you.

"For this son of mine was dead and is alive again; he was lost and is found."
Luke 15:24

Lost and Found

My Jesus,

I was selfish and prideful—I have sinned against You. I am no longer worthy of being called Your child. I've had enough; I'm coming home.

My child,

I speak to you today of My love. How I've longed for you. When you were far off, how I yearned for you. Learn a lesson from your undertakings. Faith only grows when circumstances are difficult, and you finally put your trust in Me.

When the prodigal son returned, I did not shame or embarrass him. I loved him. I put a robe around his shoulders (to keep him warm), a ring on his finger (to show him he was a valuable and priceless creation), and gave him new shoes so that he could walk unencumbered into the new life I had for him).

So it is with you, I do not condemn you. I have been waiting anxiously for your return, filled with compassion and love. I have only good things waiting for you. Step into your new freedom not weighed down with past sins. I forgave you, and I love you. A whole new world awaits you.

"We have escaped like a bird from the fowler's snare;
the snare has been broken,
and we have escaped."
Psalm 124:7

I Bring You Out

My Jesus,

The memories of my past torment me. My anxious thoughts paralyze me. I am stuck in confusion.

My child,

I am here to bring you out! Out of sorrow and regret, heartbreak over days gone by. Look to Me, look only to Me. Even as I led the Israelites out of the bondage they suffered in Egypt, I will loose you from the chains holding you captive. Reach for all that I have for you, reach for the future even though it is hidden now. The Israelites didn't know where they were going, but they so wanted to be free of captivity, they followed.

Just as the slave drivers imprisoned the Israelites, your past has imprisoned you. You can't grasp the purpose I have for you if you don't release what you're holding onto. My child, it's time to move forward.

Imagine you're climbing a ladder. You must step off one rung before stepping onto the next. If you don't, you won't move upward. It's time to let go of what you're holding onto.

161

Open your hands as if you were releasing a baby bird into the sky for the first time. To hold on would be to rob it of its future. Now imagine you are that baby bird. See yourself flying away from all that's been holding you. You will soar into all that awaits, out of the darkness into the light of freedom.

"We are afflicted in every way, but not crushed; perplexed, but not driven to despair; persecuted, but not forsaken; struck down, but not destroyed."
2 Corinthians 4:8–9 (NRSV)

Be Determined

My Jesus,

Can't it be easier? I sometimes want to give up; life is too hard.

My child,

If I could make it easier, I would, but then you would never grow. You don't get to the top of the mountain by standing at the bottom, looking up and wishing you were there. You have to take the first step.

Don't think someone will knock on your door with instructions for the rest of your life. You have to do something—move out in faith. Get up, try new things, and raise your hands to Me. Release your grasp on things you're holding onto. Maybe those things are holding you? I am bending down to lift you up. I am here.

Lazarus had to die before I could raise him. What in your life needs to die before you can be raised to the new life you desire?

Don't be concerned about what others do. Many are in the world and have pledged no allegiance to Me. Lift them to me and move on.

Start where you are. I am with you always.

I'm Already There

My Jesus,

Why am I downcast and disturbed when Your Word says I should be full of joy? Why is the road so difficult? Why am I frightened when You say I should not fear? Why am I worried about tomorrow when You tell me not to be anxious? Why can I encourage everyone else, and my world is falling apart?

My child,

You are climbing a steep mountain called life. It is challenging, demanding, and sometimes infused with pain. As you struggle to reach the top, there is a possibility of falling. Many obstacles are along your path. It's a daily challenge to look to Me, your guide. Seek Me always and speak to your mountains and stand strong.

Say to depression, "I'm replacing you with joy." Say to worry, "I'm trading you for trust." And say to anxiety, "I'm exchanging you for faith."

You may go into a valley, where you're isolated, and it's lonely. The mountains of difficulty rise high on every side, and there seems to be no way out. This is the time to keep your focus on Me and follow closely. I am leading and My helping hand is available to you to lift you over the difficulties. If I only lead you to mountain top experiences, would your faith grow? If a toddler was carried everywhere, would he learn to walk?

Remember the things I have done. Have I ever failed you? I am about to do a new thing. When you step into tomorrow, I'm already there. Look for Me in your broken dreams. You will find Me.

"But blessed is the one who trusts in the LORD, whose confidence is in Him."
Jeremiah 17:7

Are You on the Road?

My Jesus,

Where are You, Lord? I feel so alone.

My child,

I am here, though I am sometimes hidden in the everyday, mundane things of your life. After My crucifixion, the disciples went back to their regular jobs of fishing. When I came to them, they didn't recognize Me.

Or consider the two travelers on the road to Emmaus. They were sad because they thought all hope was lost. All their dreams were shattered. My Father kept them from recognizing Me for a time. They were expecting Me to do the extraordinary, not aware that I was walking with them as they lived life. Walking, such a normal thing. They weren't looking for or expecting Me, but I was there, doing an ordinary thing with them.

Are you looking for the extraordinary and not seeing Me in your everyday life? When you are disappointed and discouraged, stay on the road ahead of you, putting one foot ahead of the other. If I hide away, it is for your growth. I am building your faith.

You can find Me in the dreary, boring things of everyday life. Search for Me, and you will find Me.

"Jesus was in the stern, sleeping on a cushion. The disciples woke Him and said to Him, 'Teacher, don't you care if we drown?'"
Mark 4:38

Hold On

My Jesus,

I feel like I'm adrift on the open ocean, drifting aimlessly, tossed from one wave to the next. If You don't come to me, my heart will drown in despair in the depths of the sea. Where are You, Lord? Don't You care?

My child,

Listen to the silence of the ocean and hear My voice in the distance, calling your name. I am coming to you, walking on the waters of your pain to rescue you and save you. Reach out to Me like a drowning man would reach to his rescuer.

I am whispering words of love to you. I cherish you. You will make it. Hold on to hope. Hold on to faith. But most of all, hold on to Me. I am holding on to you.

"Finally, be strong in the Lord and in His mighty power."
Ephesians 6:10

Enemy at Hand

My Jesus,

Why am I so worn down? It seems like this battle never ends. It goes from one thing to the next. Help me, Jesus!

My child,

You are in a battle, and the enemy is trying to steal from you. He may try to steal your child, your health, or your property. He is a ruthless thief.

Think of it this way: If you came home and found your house had been broken into, you wouldn't look around and say, "Oh, he took the TV but at least he left my jewelry." No! He has no right to anything of yours. And he is ultimately after your most prized possessions: your peace and joy. If he can't get those, he can't get to you. Stand guard over your heart. Don't allow worry or fear to enter.

All the weapons you need are readily available to you, and they are mighty. Don't sit idly by while Satan deceives you. Remember, he is a liar and a thief. Be alert. Be aware. Arm yourself daily with the weapons I provide and, above all, stand strong!

Don't stop! Keep moving, go forward, and enjoy the life I have provided for you.

"For our struggle is not against flesh and blood, but against the rulers, against the authorities, against the powers of this dark world and against the spiritual forces of evil in the heavenly realms."
Ephesians 6:12

Guard Your Heart

My Jesus,

I want to be content with only You, but I am distracted by so many things. I become incapable of doing the things I know I should do, like spending quiet time with You. I want to but I feel trapped by this constant pull to do other things.

My child,

I am calling you to come, to rest in My presence. Bow low in worship and praise. The pull of this world is strong and deceiving. To stay powerful, you must guard these quiet times with all your heart. The enemy knows that as you spend time in My presence, you are renewed with new passion, more zeal, and greater love.

He will use the distractions and noise of the world to lure you away. If he can get you absorbed in things the world offers, he has won. He will attempt to get you to focus on carnal things rather than the spiritual.

The enemy is a liar. He will tell you that you're not good enough. He is a cunning master at deception. He will whisper to you that nothing you do matters. He will present you with activities that seem so worthwhile and all the time they keep you from time with Me. Be on guard for his devices!

Remember who you are. You are in this world, but you are not of this world. Speak these words out of your mouth, "I am more than a conqueror through Him who loves me." Say it over and over until it becomes real to you. I already defeated the enemy—remind him!

"Create in me a pure heart, O God, and renew a steadfast spirit within me."
Psalm 51:10

Return to Me

My Jesus,

I've turned away from You. The world has drawn me away, and darkness surrounds me. Draw me close to You again.

My child,

My heart aches for My children. So many have grown complacent and lukewarm. I am no longer their first love. I am calling, but they do not hear. I am waiting but they do not come.

Many have been lured away by the deceitfulness of this world. They are not even aware of it as they drift away so quietly, as they fade into the darkness all around them. They are in danger of becoming what they say they abhor.

So, watch over your heart with all diligence. It will grow cold unless you stay close. Stay close to the One who loves beyond measure, close to the One who protects you from dangers all around, and close to the One who gave His life for you.

Guard against becoming indifferent to Me, to My Word, or to the mission I have called you to do. The enemy will use anything he can to draw you away. Do not give him room. Rebuke him in My name, and seek a fresh anointing.

I need you to be strong in these last days. Stop what you are doing and listen for My voice. I am calling for you, as a father calls for his child when it's time to come in, out of the cold, out of the darkness. It's time to come home.

"Cast your cares on the LORD and He will sustain you; He will never let the righteous be shaken."
Psalm 55:22

Sacrifice of Praise

My Jesus,

How I long to serve You, but I feel so weak. Sometimes I let the pain of this life get to me, forgetting for a moment who You are.

My child,

During your pain, disappointment, and suffering, turn to Me and present a sacrifice of praise. Then watch as your worries fade into the distance, becoming a mist, an offering to Me. When you don't release your cares to Me, they become a weight, an anchor pulling you down. But as you release your burdens and give them to Me, you can move on, unencumbered by the cares of this world. Only then are you free, able to minister to others.

*"He turned the desert into pools of water and the parched ground into flowing **springs**."*
Psalm 107:35

Look to Jesus

My Jesus,

I am like a spring of water that has dried up, no longer able to offer refreshment to the thirsty. I lie scorched by the sun, hardened by life. I long to be an oasis in the desert that gives refreshing water to the needy, but I have nothing to offer. Why am I depleted? Why can't I hear Your voice? Help me listen with ears tuned away from worldly distractions constantly beckoning me.

My child,

You are like a car trying to run on empty or a computer that has been unplugged from its power source. I am the only source of power you need, and you have drifted away. Come back to Me, come seeking, and come daily. Come because I love you and you love Me. Sit quietly beside Me, drink in all that I am. Be filled with My Holy Spirit, and then you can give to others.

I do not require your service. When you seek Me above all else, I will show you the way. I shall provide everything you will need. No need to fret or be anxious. Only live close to My heart and watch as I direct your path. Let go of the regret and the hidden sin of pride.

Forget about yourself and rise up. Praise Me in spite of your feelings. Forget the past and move forward.

Move forward, continually knowing I am with you. Come with your arms lifted up, hands wide open to receive all I have, My promises and My love. I will be near you, and you shall be glad. Put your hope in Me.

"You make known to me the path of life; You will fill me with joy in Your presence, with eternal pleasures at Your right hand."
Psalm 16:11

Uncertain Path

My Jesus,

I don't want to go this way. It's dark, and I can't see the path ahead of me. My head is spinning as I look around, searching uselessly for a way of escape. I want to follow You Lord, but I'm scared, frightened of the unknown. Give me the strength to obey!

My child,

You say, Lord, I'll do whatever You ask, but what if I'm asking you to give up a dream? The apostles had a dream of Me restoring the kingdom to Israel. When I was taken from them, their hopes were crushed. What human wisdom could not have anticipated Calvary?

So, I say to you, though the way seems uncertain, stay close to Me. I will show it to you, little by little. I am the light that illuminates your path, unknown to you but not to Me. Step-by-step, day by day, walk by faith. Follow closely and do not stray. I am ever at your side, and I will never fail you. I am doing a new thing. A glorious future awaits.

"When I consider Your heavens, the work of Your fingers, the moon and the stars,
which You have set in place, what is mankind that You are mindful of them,
human beings that You care for them?"
Psalm 8:3–4

Wake to Thankfulness

My Jesus,

I can only weep with praise as I consider Your majesty. As I gaze at the night sky and consider the vastness of the heavens, the moon, and the stars traveling in perfect order, declaring Your glory, my thoughts are lost in admiration and wonder. I am overcome with awe. Your greatness overwhelms me. I am so tiny compared to the vastness of Your creation. Who am I that You should care for me?

My child,

I care deeply for you. You are precious to Me and I need you. You were lost, and I found you, and I long to draw you closer and closer. My love is constant. Come to Me often. Seek a fresh anointing and allow My Spirit to fill you to overflowing. Receive all that I have for you—for as freely as you receive; you are to freely give. You are My messenger to the lost.

Tell others of My love. Encourage them and speak words of hope. People are starving for hope, and many are afraid. Tell them to come out of the shadows. I am waiting to forgive their sins, erase the past, and give their life meaning and purpose. Tomorrow will be a new beginning.

"Oh, that I had the wings of a dove!
I would fly away and be at rest."
Psalm 55:6

Don't You Care?

My Jesus,

Don't You hear me, Lord, as I cry to You? I just want out! I want to fly far away from where no one knows me and hide. I want to be free from the chaos. But even in my torment, I know You will help me. My heart belongs to You.

My child,

I hear you when you call. Cast all your cares on Me, and I will sustain you (Psalm 55:22). There is nothing you're going through that I am not aware of. Don't trouble yourself with things beyond your understanding, be it a person or situation. Do not allow yourself to become bitter, worrying about how things are unraveling. And don't lock yourself in the prison of resentment.

Leave the situation in My care. I will deal with it at the right time. Now I speak peace to you, My child. This is only for a season. Put your trust in Me and move on. I have much for you to do.

Grace That
Overflows

"The LORD will guide you always; he will satisfy your needs in a sun-scorched land and will strengthen your frame."
Isaiah 58:11

Just Keep Moving

My Jesus,

I am weary, this battle is too long, and I want to be with You now.

My child,

You are stronger than you think you are, and I need you here, right where you are. You are equipped to overcome anything the enemy brings against you. You are My child, and you have My Spirit within you as a guide. Do not feel you are helpless against the enemy. You are not.

Remember, greater is He that is in you (and My Spirit is within you) than he that is in the world (1 John 4:4). Rise up in My power. I have not left you to find your own way in this world. My Word is your instruction manual.

Learn to see circumstances with spiritual eyes and fight them with spiritual weapons. You are not fighting against others but against an unseen enemy who steals, kills, and destroys. You have My Holy Spirit's power to resist anything the enemy brings against you.

The world is against Me. Stay away from anything contrary to My Word. This is a growing up time. Be easy on yourself. Move ahead slowly. I am right beside you, to hold you, to lift you, and to carry you if necessary.

Desperate for You

My Jesus,

In Your presence is fullness of joy, and I am desperate for You. I need you now, more than ever. Fall fresh on me, renew and revive me. I put my hope in You. There is no other. I bow low in worship, longing for You.

My child,

Come away with Me. Come near to Me and let Me hold you. I long for your closeness as much as you long for Mine. Quiet your racing mind as you settle into My presence. Let Me speak peace to you. Don't look to the world for validation. Look only to Me. Become familiar with My character and My ways, and you will change. You will be like a rosebud that blossoms in the springtime.

Intimate contact with Me daily will give you the assurance that all is well, and you will come to realize how very much I love you. I want only the best for you. Come now.

"That is why, for Christ's sake, I delight in weaknesses, in insults, in hardships, in persecutions, in difficulties. For when I am weak, then I am strong."
2 Corinthians 12:10

Amazing Grace

My Jesus,

Where are You Lord, when my world is falling apart?

My child,

You are experiencing growing pains—growing pains of spiritual growth. When I led the Israelites to the Promised Land, I did not lead them the shortest, easiest way. They wandered through the desert, not knowing what was ahead of them. I led them by a cloud. When the cloud moved, they moved. When the cloud didn't move, they remained where they were.

Just as I led them with a cloud to show the way, I am leading you with My Holy Spirit. Are you willing to wait for My Holy Spirit to move, or are you grumbling and complaining as the Israelites did when the going got hard? Their complaining, like a virus, affected the whole camp just as your attitude affects those closest to you.

You are climbing a mountain, and you're not on an easy path. I could have led you on an easier way but only when you have to travel through valleys, climb over boulders, and scale rocks will you become stronger, more resilient, and able to face whatever comes at you in the future. You are carving your way through the wilderness of life.

185

It's tempting to give up and quit but I, your guide, encourage you to press on, through the valley. I am with you. Rely on My strength, not your own. My grace is all you need.

"May the God of hope fill you with all joy and peace as you trust in him, so that you may overflow with hope by the power of the Holy Spirit."
Romans 15:13

Dress Rehearsal

My Jesus,

Why am I afraid of what's to come? I don't even sense I'm Your child. I feel like I'm walking into a brick wall of unbelief. Where do I get the peace You promise?

My child,

You do not know the future. I shield it from you with mercy. The days loom ahead like a book about to be written, a road about to be traveled, or a vacant house about to be entered with many rooms to explore. Open the door and follow Me.

Only by staying close will you make your way in the darkness, not only the darkness of the unknown but through the darkness in this world. Shut out the confusion and come away with Me, ridding yourself of anything that might grieve My Spirit. Guard against the fear of the unknown and do not become distracted by the world's ways. The enemy is tormenting you with thoughts of failure. He wants to confuse you and cause you to doubt My love and keeping power. Stand against all thoughts of defeat and loss.

Be still. Only in calmness and quietness will you absorb My refreshing. I long to encourage and bless you. Don't worry about anything, pray, and rise up with thanksgiving and praise, then My peace will guard your heart (Philippians 4:6).

Your life so far has been a dress rehearsal for a play that's about to begin.

"For though the righteous fall seven times, they rise again,
but the wicked stumble when calamity strikes."
Proverbs 24:16

Mercy of God

My Jesus,

I want only to do Your will, but I am fearful of the unknown. I like to think I would step out into uncharted territory to be a warrior for You, but I am weak, and my sins are many. I am plagued with regret and shame for my many failures. I am tormented, and my sin is always before me.

My child,

You need not be afraid. When the enemy plants fear, doubt, and guilt in your heart, remember, he has been defeated. You are the victor, and you have the stronger weapons. Rise up!

Imagine yourself gathering together the sins still tormenting you. Lay them at My feet, one by one, and speak freedom over them. You will never receive My gift of forgiveness while you are clutching bitterness and regret. Holding on is prideful. You are saying you doubt My forgiveness.

Trying to free yourself from unrighteousness, by acts of contrition, is like trying to free yourself from quicksand. The more you struggle, the deeper you sink.

Become steadfast in your faith and lean on Me. See yourself as a mighty victor. And don't be afraid; I am here to help you.

"Hear me, LORD, and answer me, for I am poor and needy."
Psalm 86:1

Empty Your Cup

My Jesus,

My hopes are shattered, like glass falling on the floor. Help me, Jesus, I don't know which way to go or what to do. I am disheartened and discouraged by all the wrong things I've done.

My child,

The enemy is deceiving you with thoughts of failure and regret. Accept My love and forgiveness and move on. Do not allow the enemy to deceive you any longer. You're wasting precious time when you give in to his lies. Do not be dispirited; be secure in who you are, loved and forgiven. You are My ambassador, right where you are.

See yourself strong. Purge discouragement and despair from your life. If they try to return, imagine a "closed forever" sign hanging on the door of your heart. My hope, My love, My joy and, most of all, My mercy are all available to you. Accept them by faith. You are free from your past transgressions. Walk in the freedom I purchased for you with My blood.

Put your hope in Me and walk in the light you have. Do good while you are able. I made you for great things—things only you can do, and you are greatly needed.

Don't misdirect your life and sabotage everything I have for you. Don't listen to the lies of the enemy, who will do anything to keep you from experiencing My best for you. Walk on with Me in freedom. You are destined for great things.

Endless Journey

My Jesus,

I don't think I can go on another step. I am so tired, worn down, and drained. I am empty, depleted like a balloon whose air is slowly seeping out, floating aimlessly in the sky. Where will I land? Will this never end?

My child,

There are no shortcuts to victory. You are traveling a long, seemingly endless road, and you are weary. You must take the time to refresh yourself.

Come outside and discover the beauty all around you. The garden is a retreat from the world's chaos. Breathe in its fragrance. Some flowers, like you, have been planted in the dark, deep earth, hidden from sight and isolated. After they are secluded from the world, at the right time, they spring forth and blossom as beautiful tulips and daffodils. Watch as they silently sway in the breeze, their aroma telling you there is hope. Listen for the cooing pigeons in the garden, as they whisper peace to you. I provide the scenery to be a diversion and reprieve from the weight you are carrying. Don't neglect these times of refreshment.

On the darkest day in history, Jesus carried a heavy cross, and for one brief moment, His burden was lifted as Simon helped carry His weary load. It gave Him a reprieve, so He could complete the task in front of Him. Continue on with the task in front of you, remembering I am with you to lift your burden and walk with you.

"Let us not become weary in doing good, for at the proper time we will reap a harvest if we do not give up."
Galatians 6:9

Hold Fast

My Jesus,

Give me the grace to make it through one more day. I can barely hold on. I am floating aimlessly in the ocean, bobbing up and down on the waves of depression, hopelessness, and anxiety. I'm sinking beneath the weight of my pain. I don't know the way home.

My child,

I am the way to your future, the course you must travel as you approach your final destination. Sadly, you must go through this constant, never-ending stream of heartache; there is no other way.

Look beyond these temporary trials, look beyond the pain. And when you do, cling to Me as one clings to a life preserver when they have been swept from their boat of comfort and security into the never-ending sea of disappointment. I have wrapped My arms around you to buoy you up.

Even though I don't silence the storm, I am here to get you through it. Your job is to trust. Soon, at the proper time, you will be an inspiration to many, and out of your life will spring countless blessings. Hold fast, seek Me in constant prayer, and walk on in the power of My Holy Spirit.

"For we are God's handiwork, created in Christ Jesus to do good works, which God prepared in advance for us to do."

Ephesians 2:10

Relinquish All to Me

My Jesus,

Here I am, on my knees again, desperate for You. I am here, worshiping, as my heart is breaking. I hunger for You; hear my cry and speak to me now. I am empty, desiring You to fill me with more of You than ever before, especially now in my time of dire need.

My child,

I long to fill you more than you long to be filled. Together we will press onward, leaving the past behind. I would say to you, come away with Me, find a place away from the world's chaos, and sit quietly. Be still and rest as a bird settles into its nest. I will meet you there and give you peace. Open your hands to Me, relinquish all you're holding onto, and I will fill you to overflowing. Take My hand as we walk together, out of the darkness and into the light.

Raise your voice to Me in praise, and rejoice in this new day. I will lift your cares, and I will bring you through. I will fill you with joy and a sense of peace you never would have known if it were not for this time of trial and struggle.

You are My handiwork, and I am molding you into a new creation. You will face the future with new-found courage and strength, born only in the trials of life.

"He who was seated on the throne said, 'I am making everything new!'"
Revelation 21:5

Rise above the Storm

My Jesus,

This is so unfair. I don't understand. Why did You let this happen?

My child,

Just as a jet flies above the turbulence and birds ascend beyond the tempest, you, too, must rise above the storm that's threatening you. Maybe it's the storm of sorrow and heartache and the tears won't subside. Let Me comfort you. Maybe it's the storm of guilt over what you did or didn't do; the memories are ever-present and relentless. Let Me release you from the torment. Maybe it's the storm of regret over what you should have done and didn't do and now it's too late. The downpour is ruthless and unforgiving. Let Me encourage you.

These storms are ever-present and unyielding in their intensity, but, like any cloudburst, they are only temporary. When storms rage all around you, and you think you'll never make it, run to Me. Enter into your secret place and be still.

Rest in the calmness of My presence and allow Me to allay your fears. Come, rest in My arms. Sleep peacefully knowing I make all things new, and a new day is dawning! (Ecclesiastes 11:7)

"He said to her, 'Daughter, your faith has healed you. Go in peace and be free from your suffering.'"
Mark 5:34

Run to Me

Oh, Jesus,

Here I am again, but I have nothing to offer You. I shouldn't even be here. I want to run away. Things are getting worse, and I'm exhausted.

My child,

You do not need to offer me anything except your heart. Sit with Me a while; let Me comfort you. Don't run away from me; run to Me. How I long for your visit, even if you only sit and drink in My presence and say not a word. I long for the fellowship we once had.

Deep within, you long for Me but fear renewing our relationship. Other things have slowly taken the place of your first love, and you have become distant. I know the past, and you need to leave it in the past. I hold the future in My hands, and I have planned wonderful things for you and a life anchored in Me.

There was a woman who reached out, in spite of the crowd, to touch My garment. She needed physical healing as you need spiritual healing. I told her that her faith had made her well. I would say the same thing to you.

Hear these words, My child, and come to Me. I wait patiently for you.

"Take the anointing oil and anoint him by pouring it on his head."
Exodus 29:7

Seek the Fresh Anointing

My Jesus,

I am discouraged, dejected, and so lost and alone on this journey. I am surrounded by people unaware of how I feel. If they knew, they wouldn't know what to say. Some would slip away rather than feel uncomfortable with my pain.

I was rejected—what can I do with that? I can't move forward. I don't know which way to go. There is no place to turn. My head is spinning. I am without hope. Do for me what I cannot do for myself. Give me the strength to get through one more day.

My child,

You can't change the past or see what's ahead of you. Therefore, you must turn your back on what was and walk toward the light. The further you get toward the light, your future, the more the past rejection will fade; it will become only a memory. An amazing life to come awaits you. Move forward.

Don't look to others for encouragement. They cannot meet your needs. Only I know the secrets of the heart, so open your mind and soul to Me. I will pour fragrant oil over you, a fresh anointing, suitable for each one I send to you.

Remember, I stood alone, rejected by those closest to me. At the time of My deepest need, where was everyone? Leave all to Me. Your life is in My hands.

"Forget the former things;
do not dwell on the past. See, I am doing a new thing!"
Isaiah 43:18–19

Stretch for the Future

My Jesus,

I'm holding on for my life against the gale force winds of guilt and regret. They rage against me, and I'm bending like a reed in a hurricane. I am so ashamed. I want to run away and hide. I'm falling deeper and deeper into the chasm of despondency.

My child,

Don't run from me when you fail, run to Me. Step out of the weeds into the meadow blossoming with new life. Smell the aroma of flowers wafting through the air.

You are free as you stand in My presence. Turn your back on regret, guilt, and anguish and stretch toward the dawn. Do not dwell on the past; I am not there. Leave it all behind and follow Me. I am doing a new thing. A new destiny is waiting. Follow Me.

"Why, my soul, are you downcast? Why so disturbed within me? Put your hope in God, for I will yet praise Him, my Savior and my God."

Psalm 42:5

Why Am I Sad?

My Jesus,

Why am I so sad and discouraged? It's not supposed to end like this. I have lost all hope—nothing is left. My very life depends on You. Oh, Lord, how I need You. I can't do this on my own.

My child,

Discouragement is the destroyer of hope, and no one who hopes in Me will ever be ashamed. Reach out to Me when you are depressed and burdened. Let Me comfort you. Recall what I have done in the past and reminisce. Treasure the good things; think on those times.

See yourself walking away from the past and into the light of a new normal. When you don't understand, bring to Me the sacrifice of praise and meditate on My unfailing love. I will give you the grace to go through. Be content in not knowing.

Come to Me in your distress and allow Me to carry your burdens. You are not strong enough to bear this weary load, so release the hardship to the One who can sustain you.

I have said, and My Word is true, weeping endures for a night, but joy comes in the morning (Psalm 30:5). The dawn is breaking; be watchful.

"Turn your ear to me, come quickly to my rescue; be my rock of refuge, a strong fortress to save me."

Psalm 31:2

Without Hope

My Jesus,

I never thought I'd come to this. My dreams have been dashed on the rocks of failure and disappointment. I feel so guilty. What can I do now? I have sinned against You. I'm without purpose and hope.

My child,

You are forgiven, and you are never without hope. Don't listen to the enemy's lies. He would like nothing better than for you to quit. Don't throw away your confidence.

Learn a lesson from nature. A piece of sand in an oyster is the irritant that causes a beautiful pearl to form. Let your sin, your irritant, become your testimony.

Stop, quiet your mind, and come to Me as a child comes to her father, desiring love and comfort, not criticism. You are My child, and I do not condemn you. Are you condemning yourself?

People fall for many reasons. Maybe you took the wrong turn which caused you to skid and lose your balance. Maybe you made a wrong decision and followed an unfamiliar path. Maybe you listened to friends shouting so loud they drowned out My voice. You didn't stay focused, so you fell. You succumbed to temptation.

I am not excusing the sin, but you need healing more than condemnation. Drop your fear and guilt, and come back to me. It's not too late; it's never too late. I am working using the irritations in your life to make something beautiful.

You will fulfill your purpose. Come back to Me. I stand waiting, arms wide open.

"The thief comes only to steal and kill and destroy; I have come that
they may have life, and have it to the full."
John 10:10

Change Your Focus

My Jesus,

Turn not away from me as I lament. Nothing is going the way I planned. Cleanse me as I cry to You. I am so frustrated and feel defeated. If You turn from me, where do I go, what do I do?

My child,

I will never turn away from you, but remember, you choose your attitude. It's amazing what happens when you look for and do good. How quickly you will rise out of self-absorption! Change your focus and think about good things—things that are pure and true. Redirect your frustration into gratefulness. Look for the good. It's there for you to find.

When unexpected events happen, focus on what you know of Me, not what you don't have answers for. I am love. Rest in that love, and always be thankful. Spiritual forces are all around you seeking to disparage you because you are Mine.

You need not fear. You are endued with supernatural power, and My Holy Spirit will fight the battles for you. Don't listen to the enemy. Remember, he is a liar. He wants to steal your peace and your joy.

See yourself as strong, because, with Me, you are. Fill your mouth with praise and thanksgiving. Think about what you're thinking about. Change your frustration into gratefulness. Change your focus.

"Cast all your anxiety on him, because he cares for you."
1 Peter 5:7

Don't Miss Your Miracle

My Jesus,

Why can't I find You, Lord? Why are You hidden away?

My child,

I am here but you are unaware. Are you looking for the spectacular when the greatest gifts are sometimes hidden?

Be watchful as you travel through life. Don't become distracted and walk past your miracle. Wonders are all around. Be aware. Get to the place on your journey where you are expecting to see miracles.

The Jewish people were waiting for someone to free them. They were imagining a king to set them free from their misery. They watched and waited and totally missed the miracle of My birth. The lesson here is to open your eyes! Do you think the wise men were the only ones who saw the bright star in the sky that night?

Keep searching, keep seeking, and guard from becoming discouraged. Open doors you thought were closed. A new day is dawning.

"So I say to you: Ask and it will be given to you; seek and you will find; knock and the door will be opened to you. For everyone who asks receives; the one who seeks finds; and to the one who knocks, the door will be opened."
Luke 11:9–10

Behind the Scenes

My Jesus,

I have been praying and praying until I don't have any prayers left. I thought my prayers would be answered by now. I am so discouraged.

My child,

Take heart. Your prayers are like a sweet aroma rising to heaven. I am blessed that you care enough to give of yourself for someone else. Many times in Scripture others came seeking help for another: the centurion who came on behalf of his servant, the friends who lowered the man through the roof, the man who came on behalf of his daughter, and the woman who came for her son are just a few. I commended and honored their faith, as I honor yours.

But remember, I will never violate a person's free will. He must choose. Your part is to continue to pray, pray that everywhere he goes, circumstances around him to point to Me. Pray for laborers to come across his path who speak of Me. Push back the darkness with your prayers and your praise.

Don't lose heart, be encouraged. Keep your faith alive. Don't dig up the seeds of faith with words of unbelief. You planted the seed by speaking words of faith. You watered the seed by your prayer.

Stay in faith; be encouraged. I am working behind the scenes to accomplish more than you could ever imagine.

MUSINGS – FINAL THOUGHTS

At different times in my life, I felt the Lord speak words into my heart. I based the prayers on things that happened to me over the years. I recount those experiences here, and I pray they will bless and encourage you.

I wrote *Eternity* while on vacation in Hawaii. These words came to me early one morning as I went onto the patio, alone, and gazed at the ocean.

I penned the words to *No Greater Love* while sitting at my dining room table at 1:30 A.M. after I returned from taking my husband to the Emergency Room. He had a pulse of 120+ that wouldn't subside, and the hospital admitted him for treatment. I was home alone and scared.

Yearning Heart was written when I was a young mom, overwhelmed with daily responsibilities. The Lord gently assured me that what I was doing was just fine, even though the enemy wanted me to feel guilty (and he did a good job!).

I found *Unconditional Love* in an old Bible I had used years ago. I had penned these words in a moment of frustration, again, as a young mother with no spare time. It was the Lord comforting me, assuring me of His love, and encouraging me to be the best I could be!

Finally, I wrote A Christmas Performance while attending a recital where my sweet granddaughter was performing.

"But as it is written: 'Eye has not seen, nor ear heard, Nor have entered into the heart of man The things which God has prepared for those who love Him.'"
1 Corinthians 2:9 (NKJV)

Eternity

While vacationing in Hawaii, I woke just before sunrise and went onto the patio. As I stood on the balcony overlooking the ocean below, the picture was breathtaking! It was still dark and the stars shimmered in the night sky. The waves softly rolled on the dark water. The sweet smell of plumeria gently blew through the air. The palm trees swayed in the breeze, and a still soft wind from out of nowhere silently kissed my cheek. It was stunningly beautiful and quiet. The only sound was the gentle lapping of the waves upon the rocks below.

I stood there absorbing the grandeur of the moment and was filled with awe and gratitude. I whispered, "Thank You, thank You, sweet Jesus, for creating such an amazing place! This is so gorgeous! There are no words can express how I'm feeling."

As I gazed into the darkness, I heard the Lord tenderly whisper, "My child, this is only a preview of what I have prepared for you."

"This is my comfort in my affliction, For Your Word has given me life."
Psalm 119:50 (NKJV)

No Greater Love

My Jesus,

I don't understand. Everything was fine, and now this setback! I'm feeling sad, scared, and lonely. I don't know what to do. Please help me. Please guide me.

My precious child,

Think about how much I love you. Think about Calvary. Do not allow worry to choke My Word. Claim all that is available to you to get you through, especially My peace.

When you feel uneasy, escape to that secret place with Me until I flood you with My presence. You may have to come hourly. Come as often as needed but come. Then you will be strong enough to go on, not in your strength, but in Mine. When the enemy sees you facing problems using the weapons I provide, he is defeated. Remember, My Word is your sword.

My everlasting arms are under you, holding you tightly, lifting you high above troubling circumstances of this life. Be still and rest peacefully in My arms. You are more secure than an infant cradled by his mother.

Remember to always be thankful. Praise and thanksgiving during pain honor me. Being thankful when you have yet to see the answer demonstrates your faith. Practice living one day at a time. Be comforted to know the God of the universe sees and knows what you're going through. I am charting the rough waters of this life for you. Trust Me.

"Our actions will show that we belong to the truth, so we will be confident when we stand before God. Even if we feel guilty, God is greater than our feelings, and He knows everything. Dear friends, if we don't feel guilty, we can come to God with bold confidence."
1 John 3:19–21 (NLT)

Yearning Heart

My Jesus,

How I long to spend time with You, but I so often fail. I feel like I am being pulled in one thousand directions! So many things need my attention! I don't even take time to pray, and I feel so guilty.

My precious child,

I see your struggles, but I also see your heart, and I know it seeks Me. Pursue My help constantly throughout the day. Allow your family and your daily activities to be your prayer, offering them to Me with a joyful heart. A life well-lived honors Me. Make it your goal to enjoy every day. It is My gift to you.

The enemy would like nothing more than to get you frustrated, tired, and upset. Don't waste these precious moments with regret or guilt. I speak peace to you.

Rest quietly in My love. I am for you and I will help you. In fact, I long to help you. Remember, this is the day that I have made. Say, "I will rejoice and be glad in it" (Psalm 118:24).

"When I was a child, I spoke as a child, I understood as a child, I thought as a child; but when I became a man, I put away childish things. For now we see in a mirror, dimly, but then face to face. Now I know in part, but then I shall know just as I also am known.
1 Corinthians 13:11–13 (NKJV)

Unconditional Love

My Jesus,

How I love you! I can't describe the depth of my feelings. Sometimes I feel so inadequate. I desire to know what You want of my life. Please reveal to me where I'm going and teach me to be content where I am now.

My child,

I love you with a love that's as deep as the ocean, so deep you can't even imagine how much I love you. Think of how precious and innocent a little baby is. When I look at you, you are my baby—so cherished. I want to guide and protect you just as you want to guide and protect your little one.

As you walk through this life, strive to be guided by all I've taught you. Remember, My love dictates everything I do. Go slowly, My child. Don't try to rush ahead and neglect the present. All is well. I hold everything in My hands. Just pace yourself day by day. Go forward, and, as I have told you, My grace is sufficient for you (2 Corinthians 12:9).

I am grooming you. As a gardener tends to his garden, I am

218

tending to you, My choicest flower. Again, I say, remember how much I love you. Love is all you need. Love never fails. Remember this as you interact with your family. I am holding all of you.

"And now these three remain: faith, hope and love. But the greatest of these is love."
1 Corinthians 13:13

A Christmas Performance

I attended a Christmas recital where my four-year-old granddaughter was in the chorus. I could see her clearly because I was sitting just two rows from the stage. She was so beautiful! I glanced at the other little girls around her. They all had been dressed so beautifully and were smiling sweetly. A few were squirming and quietly giggling, anxious for their big performance.

While they were all lovely, my eyes kept coming back to my little granddaughter. Every time I looked at her, my heart skipped a beat, and an overwhelming love washed over me. Though the other children were delightful, so precious and excited, the love I felt for my granddaughter was indescribable and I thought, "I would just do anything for that little one!"

Right then, I heard the Lord whisper to my heart, "My child, that's the kind of overwhelming love I feel for you." Then I glanced at my daughter, who was sitting across the aisle. I looked at her and I thought, "Oh, my goodness, she really resembles me." Once again, I heard the Lord whisper, "My child, when people look at you, would they say you resemble Me?"

"But they that wait upon the LORD shall renew their strength; they shall mount up with wings as eagles; they shall run, and not be weary; and they shall walk, and not faint."

Isaiah 40:31 KJV

About the Author

Judy lives in southern California with her husband, Greg. She has four married daughters, four outstanding sons-in-law and the most amazing grandchildren you'll ever meet!

She worked as a registered nurse and she spent most of her professional life working in the mental health field. After leaving nursing, she found a new vocation—volunteering at her church in the counseling ministry.

She had no intention of being a writer. She journaled for years and when she shared some writings at various venues, many people were blessed and inspired. Those same people urged her to share God's words by "writing a book" so that others could be encouraged. You are holding that book in your hands.

www.ingramcontent.com/pod-product-compliance
Lightning Source LLC
Chambersburg PA
CBHW061142040426
42445CB00013B/1515